INISHKILLANE

By the same author

Maps and Dreams

INISHKILLANE
Change and Decline in the West of Ireland

HUGH BRODY

faber and faber
LONDON · BOSTON

First published in 1973 by Allen Lane
This edition published in 1986 by
Faber and Faber Limited
3 Queen Square London WC1N 3AU

Printed in Great Britain by
Redwood Burn Limited, Trowbridge, Wiltshire and
bound by Pegasus Bookbinding, Melksham, Wiltshire
All rights reserved

© Hugh Brody 1973

British Library Cataloguing in Publication Data

Brody, Hugh
    Inishkillane: change and decline in the
    West of Ireland.
    1. Ireland—Social conditions 2. Ireland
    —Rural conditions
    I. Title
    941.7'009'734   HN398.17

    ISBN 0-571-14582-5

Contents

List of Figures

List of Tables

Did not my mistake, and that of my profession, lie in the belief that men are not always men? That some are more deserving of our interest and our attention because there is something astonishing to us in their manners, or in the colour of their skins? No sooner are such people known or guessed at, than their strangeness drops away, and one might as well have stayed in one's own village.

Claude Lévi-Strauss: *World on the Wane*

Oh hand in hand, let us return to the land of our birth, the bogs, the moors, the glens, the lakes, the rivers, the streams, the brooks, the mists, the – er – fens, the – er – glens, by tonight's mail-train.

Samuel Beckett: *Murphy*

SCALE 1:2 250 000

0   50m
0   80km

TORY I.

DONEGAL

LONDONDERRY

ANTRIM

TYRONE

ULSTER

belfast

FERMANAGH

ARMAGH

DOWN

SLIGO

LEITRIM

MONAGHAN

ACHILL I.

MAYO

ROSCOMMON

CAVAN

LONGFORD

LOUTH

MEATH

CONNAUGHT

WESTMEATH

LEINSTER

GALWAY

galway

OFFALY

dublin

DUBLIN

ARAN IS

GALWAY BAY

KILDARE

LEIX

WICKLOW

CLARE

shannon

CARLOW

limerick

KILKENNY

BLASKET I.

LIMERICK

TIPPERARY

WEXFORD

MUNSTER

WATERFORD

KERRY

CORK

cork

BANTRY BAY

Political Map of Ireland

Acknowledgements

My research in the west of Ireland was financed by the Social Science Research Council of Great Britain and Trinity College, Oxford. Mr John Wright and Dr David Goldey were of invaluable help in the beginning of the project when the odds against it seemed overwhelming. Dr Brian Wilson has over a number of years been extremely generous with his time in reading and criticizing a multitude of preliminary drafts. Bob Sutcliffe, Brian Trench, and Arnold Cragg all made many perceptive and constructive comments on the final draft as well as continuously encouraging me in the work. I must also thank Alison Soskice for help with compiling census data, Howard Copping for drawing up graphs and tables, and Jackie Allwood for all her help in preparing the manuscript for the publishers. Special thanks are due to Andrew Kimmens, but for whose painstaking comments on every page of the manuscript the whole would have been even less satisfactory.

But the great debt is of course to the people of the west of Ireland, the men and women who offered me their incomparable hospitality, and so openly talked to me of life in their countryside. They are not people who would welcome their names in print, but if they read this they must know that but for them the whole would have lacked substance in the reporting and pleasure in the doing.

In order to preserve the anonymity of those who befriended

me in Ireland I have changed the name of the parish. I have altered details of its history and played endless tricks on geography. Strictly speaking Inishkillane does not exist. Unfortunately many hundreds of parishes very much like it do.

London, April 1971

The preparation of this new edition of *Inishkillane* has not been easy. More than ten years have passed since it was first written. Inevitably, it now seems to me to be caught by its own particular moment; and I suspect that were I to write it now, the whole text would be very different. In its way, however, I believe the book has stood the test of time, and I am grateful to Neil Middleton, Jill Norman and Tom Engelhardt for persuading me that it should be republished.

I have reworked and then added to the introductory chapter. The rest, however, is unaltered. This must mean that changes in the world, changes that have borne sharply on every part of Irish life, are not matched by a suitably new text. Nor have I taken detailed account of the book's critics. Nonetheless, on recent visits to the places I first stayed in the west of Ireland, I was so forcefully reminded of the findings and ideas out of which this book first grew that its republication seemed to be justified. There are still many hundreds of parishes very much like Inishkillane.

So once again I must acknowledge the great debt I owe to the people of the west of Ireland. Their openness and forthrightness continue to amaze me: many of them have every good reason to be sceptical about, if not simply hostile to, an English writer. And it is to Kate Nee, on behalf of all the people who helped me in every way, that I dedicate this new edition of the book.

London, April 1982   *Hugh Brody*

Introductory
White Stockings on Burned Heels

I first visited the west coast of Ireland in early spring, 1966. It was to the home of Kate Nee, then a woman of sixty maintaining entirely on her own a small mountain farm in Connemara, that I had been directed by an old friend of Kate's living in England. Kate Nee was not in her house when I arrived, and I began to walk round to the vegetable garden at the back, looking for some sign of her. Suddenly she appeared, walking down the hillside with a pail of milk, black shawl draped around her shoulders. Nervously I began to explain who I was, but no sooner had I said the friend's name than Kate cried, 'My darling!', clasped me in a tight hug, and hurried to make the first of a thousand teas.

Reading Maurice O'Sullivan's *Twenty Years A-Growing* had drawn me to Ireland, most particularly to the west. So when Kate showed how beautifully she could lilt a Gaelic air, or pushed aside her kitchen furniture to make room for a jig, or sat on the seat at the edge of a turf fire to tell long stories of her life in the country and of its people, or showed the best music to sing while milking a troubled cow, it seemed sure that expiry of life on the Great Blasket Island, postscript to Maurice O'Sullivan's reminiscences, could not be the symbol of change in rural Ireland.

But Kate Nee was alone on her land, with no heir in the house to follow her, and with sons and daughters living in London, Yorkshire, Chicago, New York, Arizona and Los Angeles. Three of her children died in infancy; nine emigrated; and only one – her oldest daughter – married a local farmer, and remained in Ireland. After the birth of her thirteenth child, Kate's husband went to work in England; it was the beginning of the Second World War, and he found a job in a munitions factory. Life was not easy for him there, living in a cheap boarding house instead of on his own farm in Connemara. Kate sent him extra food, but on his trips home to Ireland she noticed that he was beginning to look ill. Then, during one Christmas visit home, he told Kate that he thought his health was indeed failing. Still, he went back to his job and boarding house – only to return to Connemara a few months later. Kate took him to Galway hospital, where he died. Subsequently the children emigrated themselves. By the time I first met her, Kate Nee had been alone for eight years. Nor was Kate's story untypical. In 1966 four families lived within a mile of her house; fifty years before there had been thirty.

After five years of work, and after visits to many other parts of the Irish countryside, and after prolonged stays – working on farms, in fishing boats, as barman – my picture of the remoter communities of Ireland was related as much by its opposition as by its similarity to the Blaskets and Connemara of Maurice O'Sullivan and Kate Nee. At about the time I began this book the country's population had fallen to its lowest point since reliable censuses began – from eight million in 1841 to four million in 1961.* The strength and vitality of Irish peasant society could not endure this kind of population decline, or the economic and political forces by which it was caused; least of all could the peasant society of the west, where population decline was experienced in its most extreme and destructive form, do other than lament – perhaps with all manner of romantic nostalgia – a way of life that seemed to be dying.

*This is a round figure for the whole of Ireland. The 1961 population of Eire alone was just over 2,800,000.

During the years I lived and worked in the west, I came to know three communities that were for the most part bilingual, the Irish spoken as much as the English, with far more Irish in the privacy of family and home. Two of these communities are in Donegal and one is in Galway. But a parish in West Clare and a parish in West Cork, both exclusively English speaking, became the centres of my work. In sociological terms, this work was participant observation: I lived in the communities as a visitor or additional hand, never as an investigator. No interviews were ever set up, and no formal questionnaires ever undertaken with the people as a whole or even with any section of a community. The 'hard' data – most particularly the statistics used in Chapter 3 – come from parish records, from Dublin offices of rates and land commission, and from the helpfulness of official people, especially priests, doctors and teachers. In these different ways I came to a much fuller knowledge of the west of Ireland, and came to see the intense demoralization affecting so many of its people.

In coming to a view of the countryside which places weightiest emphasis on the decline of community and increase of despondency in the people, I realized that the processes at work in the parishes and households where I lived were part of changes affecting a much broader area than the remote corners of Ireland. Changes in farming practice, re-evaluation of rural life, inter-family and inter-personal relationships, the consciousness of the young – all these extend an account of Ireland into more general issues.

Yet at the heart of any work dealing with Ireland, either in its more recent changes or during the periods of supposedly most stable traditional life, must lie the country's own literature. I have already mentioned Maurice O'Sullivan; he is one of several writers who have described in detail and with great beauty the peasant society that is often seen as the very basis of Irish culture. I give a bibliography of books about Ireland.

> *Clay is the word and clay is the flesh*
> *Where the potato-gatherers like mechanized*
> > *scarecrows move*
> *Along the side-fall of the hill –*
> > *Maguire and his men.*
> *If we watch them an hour is there anything*
> > *we can prove*
> *Of life as it is broken-backed over the Book*
> *Of Death? Here crows gabble over worms and frogs*
> *And the gulls like old newspapers are blown*
> > *clear of the hedges, luckily.*
> *Is there some light of imagination in these*
> > *wet clods?*
> *Or why do we stand here shivering?*
>
> Patrick Kavanagh: *The Great Hunger*

They range from reminiscences and autobiographies, through the plays and poetry of Synge, O'Casey and Patrick Kavanagh, to the Irish in exile who touch again and again the disarray and breakdown in their society. There can be no clear distinguishing between the literary and social evolutions of the country. Peig Sayers is sensitive to a traditional social heritage, yet she can no more separate what she remembers from her immediate sense of the change and disappearance of the old life than can Samuel Beckett in *Murphy* neglect to remark the confusion of migrants dissolving into London, with Murphy himself drawing ever deeper into his own private world of mind. Peig Sayers tells of a community she remembers as strong and now sees passing, while Beckett describes the privacy and isolation that follow.*

*Peig Sayers, *An Old Woman's Reflections*, Oxford University Press, 1962; Samuel Beckett, *Murphy*, London: John Calder, 1938.

The more strictly sociological literature on rural Ireland is far less rich and compelling. Country life in West Clare was the subject of a comprehensive description by Conrad Arensberg and Solon Kimball in the late 1930s.* Arensberg and Kimball spent an extended period of time in one village, and its description takes the form of an anthropological study of the most empirical kind: 'The purpose . . . is not so much to characterize the communities described as it is to examine the behaviour of the persons living in them.' However, they see Irish rural life as a distinctive culture, certainly changing, but nonetheless a highly integrated culture. Further, the conception they have of their discipline rules out all 'judgements', and equally makes anything other than a belief in the culture they are studying extremely unlikely. They emphasize its solidity and coherence in the present as well as its sure endurance in the future. Much is declared to be beyond the realm of their investigations: 'They (the authors) do not feel themselves qualified in any way to characterize or evaluate the culture, tradition or social life or the communities in which they made their study.'

Arensberg and Kimball's work is full of ethnographic detail. But their picture of Ireland is shaped, and then distorted, by the absence of historical setting: it has largely escaped the authors that the tradition they discuss was scarcely a hundred years old at the time of their work. Many of the details they emphasize, including their focal thesis of 'familism', assumed importance no earlier than 1840. Yet, in explaining the choice of Irish country life as a testing ground for functionalist hypotheses, they cite its 'long relatively unbroken tradition

*Conrad M. Arensberg and Solon T. Kimball, *Family and Community in Ireland*, Harvard University Press, 1968; also Conrad M. Arensberg, *The Irish Countryman*, Macmillan, 1937. The 1968 edition of *Family and Community in Ireland* includes the results of work carried out by the authors in an Irish town.

dating back to pre-Christian and pre-Roman times.' The error of this, especially in talking of the farm families of the west, is described here in Chapter 2. But K. H. Connell, in his brilliant essays on Ireland before and after the great famine of 1846-52, has exposed that error in all its historical ramifications.*

Arensberg and Kimball's commitment to rigid functionalism led them to confident and optimistic predictions about rural Ireland. In assiduously hunting down and underscoring the harmony of the system they came to know so well, they were hardly likely to predict disintegration or even decline. Whatever functions and is adaptable will, albeit in altered form, continue to function. Thus they tell us that 'the distinctive culture of Ireland is increasing in strength and autonomy, however much it has learned to assimilate the technological and other developments of the modern age'.

All the most compelling forces in the west of Ireland of the 1960s (no longer, if it ever was, 'the distinctive culture of Ireland'), confound that prediction. That Arensberg and Kimball were not conscious of Irish history, and regarded a social system with a span of no more than four generations as the very essence of rural Irish life, may shift complaint against functionalism itself to their particular exposition of it. But not only sociologists and anthropologists made this mistake: the writings of Synge and Yeats are also bedevilled by a romantic and idealistic conviction that the peasantry they visited in Connemara, Kerry and Galway offered a living example of pre-Christian Europe. In fact, the structure of what so many writers and politicians liked to celebrate as an ancient tradition was limited, even in the course of its short existence, by a set of contradictions and tensions. These were implicit when Synge

*The Population of Ireland, 1750-1845 (Oxford University Press, 1950) and Irish Peasant Society (Oxford University Press, 1968) include his principal theses.

It is not now as it was then, but it is like a sea on ebb, and only ponds here and there left among the rocks.

Robin Flower: *The Western Island*

travelled in the west; and they were probably emerging into the open at the time of Arensberg and Kimball's field trips.

Nonetheless, there are startling echoes of the story I try to tell in this book, echoes that can be heard in all kinds of texts that deal with Ireland and peasant life. The poetry of early Christian times, collections of myths, plays, political rhetoric, essays, and even government reports or general anthropological works seem suddenly and sharply, in some quite different idiom or at some quite other time, to illuminate or amplify what I am saying here. Perhaps in the case of Ireland literature and history are especially intertwined; certainly Irish culture and politics looked to the country's literature for self-definition. Perhaps the agonies of Irish experience demanded and found forms of protest and resistance which shaped the most passionate of modern literary traditions. For whatever mix of reasons, a sense of Ireland and a sense of writing are almost inseparable. And in this book I have allowed a sort of fragmented sub-text to appear, or erupt, through the pages. This sub-text is built from quotations, which at times interrupt and at times amplify my arguments. They are there as much for the pleasure of the reader as for any direct intellectual purpose; and if they seem to break into the flow of the main text, they can be read separately – by scanning and dipping. However they are read, they give a taste of the work done by a remarkable range of observers, from Conrad Arensberg to Brendan Behan.

Whatever these writers may say, however, the transformation of Ireland's farm communities and families has been relatively sudden. All the evidence suggests critical turning points – in the 1840s and then again in the 1930s. Emigration became endemic in the mid nineteenth century, continued until the 1970s, and in many areas is still part of Irish life. Most important, emigration on a massive scale was a feature of the social order that emerged after the famine. In West Clare, at the time of Arensberg and Kimball's investigations, young people were leaving the land in a large and steady flow. With this persistent and ineluctable movement of Irish country people into the cities of America and England, those who remained at home on the land also became implicated with urban life and capitalist economies. Flows of emigration create and nurture flows of money and information: children at work outside the country convey, in a clear and simple way by letter and the enclosed cash or postal order, the successes they have attained – or pretend to have attained – and the life they now lead. When they return for visits emigrants also demonstrate, in every way available to them, the new life they have found and its benefits.* And where leaving has required a violation of home life, a defiance of parental wishes, or – most importantly – an apparent disregard for local economic imperatives, the emigrants' accounts of their new lives produce greater and greater justifications: overstatements which portray urban life as safely flowing with milk and honey.

Yet the young men and women who left rural Ireland in the decades following the famine were more pushed out, than lured by the glitter of Chicago or London. In the same period the gap was wide between the life of a farm family in the community and the social conceptions and styles essential to urban

*The self-generating quality of rural-urban emigration has often been noted. William Peterson, for example, in 'A General Typology of Migration' (*American Sociological Review*, XXIII, 3, 1958) notes: 'Once it is well begun, the growth of such a movement is semi-automatic: so long as there are people to emigrate, the principal cause of emigration is prior emigration' (p. 263).

*I looked west at the edge of the sky where America should be lying,
and I slipped back on the paths of thought. It seemed to me now
that the New Island was before me with its fine streets and great
high houses, some of them so tall that they scratched the sky; gold
and silver out in the ditches and nothing to do but gather it. . . . I
see the boys and girls who were once my companions . . .*

Maurice O'Sullivan: *Twenty Years A-Growing*

capitalism. Although generation after generation of emigrants
was crossing the gap between ways of life, those at home maintained for a long time their confidence and faith in their own
society.

Like the rest of the Celtic fringe, rural Ireland was an object
of ruthless foreign landlordism. Indeed, the kind of peasant
landholding, farming and family life described by Arensberg
and Kimball and others were products of a long history of col-
onial exploitation. Throughout the nineteenth century landlords, helped by both agricultural policies and military actions
designed in Westminster, continued to extract whatever surplus they could from their lands and tenants. And even in the
late 1930s – at least a decade after the Irish Free State had
transformed the tenantry into owner-occupiers – Irish farm
families clung tenaciously to their land and their specialized
way of life.

This apparent stability, despite its having been formed in response to and defiance of the most intense external pressures,
could not persist indefinitely. Beneath its surfaces, the system
was fraught with internal strain. Moreover, Irish country
people, even in the outlying communities along the western
seaboard, were literate and mobile. The English had set up
National Schools in the nineteenth century, where Irish-
speaking children were drilled in English; and wave upon
wave of these English-speaking Irish had gone to live in

English-speaking countries. While nationalist leaders looked to the west for political inspiration and the basis for a new, independent identity for the Eire republic, the peasantry of the west looked to England and America for economic security. Inevitably, the consciousness of the country people began to change: it became less clear that the family farm really did represent all that was good and hopeful. By 1940 Irish culture had evolved the double nostalgia that has been one of its hallmarks: emigrants in Chicago sang heartfelt laments about home, while their younger brothers and sisters at home talked wistfully about the wonders and riches of America.

No social system is internally consistent; all must devise practices and codes of belief which minimize or obscure contradictions. This means that there are always individuals or, more likely, whole sections of a society that are responsive to the prospect of change. Once change is adumbrated, or covertly under way, those most quick to see their disadvantage in the status quo will be enthusiastic about alternatives. And as significant numbers become conscious of alternatives, they will use them as a form of very effective criticism. As a group or class, they may force change into a situation previously accepted with apparent resignation. Or they may leave.

Criticism of life at home often thus turns on comparisons. When these comparisons are with urban capitalism in its heyday, the result is a special kind of open-endedness; and home

---

The struggle for survival compels the ethnic to participate in the economy of the host society even before he participates in other spheres of its social life. Moreover, this enforced participation in the economy leads to a weakening of the ethnic social heritage which ultimately will be replaced by values of the host culture.

E. K. Francis: 'The Adjustment of a
Peasant Community to a Capitalist Economy'

---

life suffers under a special disadvantage. Capitalism represents itself as a culture of freedom, where social, sexual and economic opportunities abound. This image of personal freedom insists that anyone, if he or she is willing and in some minimal degree competent, can seize opportunities and somehow thrive. The features of the society that underpin this image are various: subordination of place of work to individual whim and profitability, an anonymous urban milieu with a multitude of distractions, perfectly adapted to a vast range of tastes and activities. The media that export this culture's account of itself carry the message – in magazines, on the cinema and television – to capitalism's remoter hinterlands, the west of Ireland among them. The people who carry the images back home are migrants. Both the media and the migrants emphasize and highlight the benefits of ways of life in the centre, in the heartlands of capitalist society. And overstatement is necessary if only because the life which emigrants in fact lead is not commensurate with the life the media and they themselves depict.

This image of capitalism is built from suggestions of opportunities that in their plethora will exclude no one. According to its account of itself, capitalist society can accommodate needs and idiosyncracies, can placate anxieties and frustrations, can make a 'good life' for anyone. Money is available to all who are willing to work; supplies can be found for any demand; advance and increase come to all who are prepared to strive within its fabric. There would thus seem to be provision for whatever detail of personality or life may seem to be undernourished at home, in the 'traditional' limiting framework of constraints and demands. It follows that the person who is captivated by images of capitalism can only find disadvantage at home, where everything is familiar, where the world is made up of cold facts. For the restless and the disadvantaged the world at home, at critical historical moments, appears inflexible and unbearably dominant; and its exactly defined future can assume the aspect of irremediable oppression.

Comparison is therefore between rigid practice in a definite place, and a milieu whose features can include whatever anyone feels he or she could do with. The imagination's map can be detailed by each according to need and frustration; and the idea of life in cities of America and England can include quite simply the absence of any source of discontent. What is bad at home is, in the imagining, just what life in London will be without. Moreover, the would-be emigrant does not have to be specific: the difficulty at home can be expressed in the most general form, as 'Home' (with a sneer). In its account of itself, then, urban capitalism appeals to the imagination's flight. And those who are most vulnerable to the real contradictions that do exist at home are typically the most imaginative.

Millions of people left Ireland. For successive generations emigration was a necessary mainstay of family farming; but in the 1930s and '40s it became, for many, a simple preference. The peasant society that emerged in the aftermath of the famine became involved in spirals of change which could not easily be checked or cushioned. This account of remote rural parishes shows how the process has roots in the way this peasant system developed, and how its course has been both swift and sure. I shall describe the reconstituted family life, the isolation of each home, the increasing loneliness of many people, and the decline of community itself. The peasant society, the way of life so tenderly described by the Gaeltacht authors of Kerry and Donegal, the culture admired and explored by Yeats and Synge, has been transformed into another kind of society.

For more than a century Irish country people helped to fight a guerrilla war against English colonists and their puppet governments in Dublin. Over the same period Irish peasant society transformed itself into a complex if ultimately untenable system. The war against England was eventually won, but

The ancient countries and traditional ways of thought and be-
haviour tend to disappear before the destroying breath of 'the spirit
of the age'. We have suffered great cultural losses as a nation, and
can ill afford to let pass unrecorded and unappreciated the spirit of
Ireland, the tradition of the historic Irish nation. It was for the old
ways of life – for the petite patrie *– that our forefathers fought and*
died, more than for kings, principalities and powers.
                Sean O'Suilleabhain: *A Handbook of Irish Folklore*

the war against England's economic order was never effectively joined. This book deals exclusively with the disarray which
the latest encounter, this time with capitalism itself and the
consciousness it creates, wrought in the Irish countryside.

So far, most of this chapter was first written in 1971. Looking back at it, and at the whole of this book, more than ten
years later, I am bound to be aware of many changes. The intense relationships between observer and observed is exposed
in retrospect; the distance between writer, at a particular
moment in personal history, and a subject, at a moment in *its*
history, is not as it previously appeared. Beyond this inevitable awareness of changes in appearances from within the text,
there are, however, comparatively simple changes in matters
of fact. There is no need to evade the question: has the book
stood the tests of time? My answer is, many of them.
   The 1971 census of Ireland showed that for the first time
since 1841 the country's population had grown. Between 1971
and 1979 the new trend continued, with the later census showing an increase of a little over 13 per cent. Most striking of all,
the 15-29 age group increased in that decade by 25 per cent.
The story had changed: flight from the land apparently was no
longer so all-pervasive.

The world had changed in ways that influenced these census findings. Recession in England and America made emigration less economically appealing. In particular, the building trades – traditional source of employment for the Irish in Britain – reflected the succession of slumps that became an economic crisis. At the same time, re-eruption of violence in Ulster resulted in a host of new powers of arrest and detention for the English police: life in England became more difficult for many Irish emigrants.

In Eire, meanwhile, entry into the European Economic Community gave rise to hopes for a revitalization of Irish farming. And if this soon became a benefit almost exclusively for large farms on good land, prospects implied by the EEC's repeated statements of forthcoming support for marginal farms were nothing if not tantalizing. At the same time, even the remotest farmlands were affected by a rapid rise in land values: Europeans looking for holiday homes drove prices for derelict cottages and agriculturally worthless or neglected plots to un-dreamed-of heights. The family farm came, quite suddenly, to have real cash value. Also, the Irish government gave support to farmers by increasing the dole: economically unviable farms received weekly help in the form of newly generous transfer payments.

Many young men and women, therefore, who in the 1960s would certainly have emigrated, in the 1970s stayed in Ireland. And many emigrants living in England, and to a lesser extent in America, returned to homes in the west. These were often couples who had children: whole families went back to farms their children had only visited during summer holidays. The scale of this move back to Ireland has been considerable: Kate Nee's granddaughter goes to an Irish-speaking Connemara school where over a third of the children were born in England.

And Kate's life has changed. In 1977 one of her sons inherited an uncle's farm – the very farm, in fact, where his father and grandfather had been born. It is a small patchwork of stony fields on the Connemara seashore. The vegetable garden behind the house has been built on rock, an accumulation of seaweed and stable manure: the bare rock is exposed between lazy-beds. But Kate's son and his wife (who also was born in County Galway) decided to move back to Ireland, bringing their English-born children with them. They had been away for over 25 years.

Then another of Kate's sons also came home. He had left Ireland as a teenager, lived in England for four years, and finally went to America. He stayed in Chicago for twenty-three years, working in an electronic components factory. He has no land of his own, and lives with his mother. Kate is no longer alone on her mountain farm.

But this bare outline of Kate's story conceals the persistence of former changes and decline, and hides regional differences. Her sons and daughter-in-law are not back in the Ireland they knew as children. They say that they nursed childhood dreams when living away, and coming back to the west they hoped to realize such dreams. Now they stand on Irish soil, on family farms, on 'the old sod', and nostalgically recall life in London, Yorkshire, Chicago . . . And their view of Ireland is still haunted by dreams: the place they remembered, or imagined, does not exist.

Has it disappeared? In some ways, they say, and agree with Kate's lament for the passing of the society in which she raised the children. There is very little visiting, almost no mutual aid; a small and scattered rural population continues to depend on the dole and pensions – along with familiar remittances from abroad. And Kate's grandchildren are unclear about whether or not there can be a future for their in the countryside.

Or did the society of childhood dreams never exist? Irish culture is strongly felt. The people and ways of life of the west are celebrated by national governments of all parties. And to-day's young people are, if anything, far more proud of being from the west of Ireland than their older siblings and parents were fifteen or twenty years ago. Yet the play between mythology and history is endemic in a country where ideas of national character and distinctive identity have had major roles in political life. The government's continuing insistence on Irish language in the country's schools, and grants of special subsidies to Irish-speaking households, are tokens of this interplay. In the end, the past and modern images of the past are inseparable.

A flat statement of the 1979 census return shows revival as a national generality. The detailed figures, however, reveal some startling regional differences. In fact, in the west and midlands of Ireland, migration was continuing at very high rates. Some parishes continued to lose population at around 10 per cent per decade; in many parishes of the west population was unchanged between 1971 and 1979. Natural increase and return of migrants were being offset by similarly large numbers of people leaving the land. Throughout the west, in fact, migration from the countryside to Irish towns appears to have taken over, in significant measure, where emigration to England left off. Moreover, the old tendency for young women to leave in larger numbers than young men persisted. In Counties Kerry and Monaghan, for example, the 1979 census shows that for every one thousand young men, there were less than 900 young women; and in County Cavan, there were less than 800. These statistics alone suggest that many of the patterns and problems found in the Inishkillane of the late 1960s have continued.

Kate Nee can evoke, with all the power that comes from an Irish speaker's use of English, an irrefutable sense of the distinctiveness of her culture. Like so many elderly people in the west of Ireland, she recreates in stories and reflections her society's ways of using land, dealing with neighbours, raising children, believing in God and the Angels, thinking about strangers, considering death, and a whole understanding of what it is to work as a woman. Each of these is lit by her awareness of difference; and in sum, as Kate knows perhaps all too clearly, therein lie both the reality of a culture and an insistence that it is all but gone.

Kate also knows that her society has been recast by emigration, and by emigrants' needs and notions. She sees how they see her, and how they are seen by strangers. But she is not sure whether her community, her Inishkillane, can offer any real advantage, or even sufficient dignity – some possible compensation for not being somewhere else. Perhaps she was once much clearer about this; or perhaps she can half remember, half imagine what it is like to be thus clear. Meanwhile, the imaginations of her sons, like all the emigrants both at home and abroad, and like Kate herself, continue to be haunted by images of other times and other places.

Much of the most poignant Irish literature has come from this imaginative displacement. Its literary forms often depend, understandably enough, on contrasts between past coherence and present demoralization. Such contrasts are often made explicit by the author – as in the case of Maurice O'Sullivan. But even when the contrasts are not detailed there is a feeling that such books or poems would not have been written were the authors not alert to the collapse of much of what they describe. Sociological accounts of change and decline in the west of Ireland inevitably appear late in the process. Peig Sayers, in her *An Old Woman's Reflections*, said in the 1930s what Kate Nee recounted in hers, and what I have tried to say in mine:

> See myself here, sitting on the fence, looking around me and thinking on the hundreds of things that are gone. I see the change that has come in life in my own memory, the importance and the snobbery. There are white stockings on the burned heels today and the back of the hand given to customs and manners of the old and alternative life being led. It can't be helped, I suppose, because life is changing as the years are passing along.

Drink was cheap too. It wasn't thirst for the drink that made us want to go where it was, but only the need to have a merry night instead of the misery we knew only too well before. What the drop of drink did to us was to lift up the hearts in us, and we would spend a day and a night ever and again in company together when we got the chance. That's all gone by now, and the high heart and the fun are passing from the world. Then we'd take the homeward way together easy and friendly after all our revelry, like the children of one mother, not doing hurt or harm to his fellow.

Thomas O'Crohan: *The Islandman*

Since the middle of the last century the livelihood of traditional Irish homes has depended, according to region and local history, on potatoes, cattle and fishing. Only in the remotest lands of the west and during the period of densest population prior to the great famine of 1846–51 did any large number of families or communities live by totally self-contained agricultural

A good season is peaceful summer;
luxuriant is the tall fine wood
which the whistle of the wind will not stir,
green is the plumage of the sheltering grove;
eddies swirl in the stream;
good is the warmth of the turf.

Sixth-century Celtic poem

subsistence. In less fertile areas and in more recent times the rural economy of even the western seaboard of Ireland has become a blend of subsistence, marketing and commercial fishing. Since the end of the nineteenth century a crucial additional ingredient has been the remittance from abroad. The livelihood of small farm families now depends upon at least two of these ingredients, and the traditional annual cycle is structured accordingly.

Around the beginning of February, at the time marked on the religious calendar by St Brigid's Day, each family began to prepare the land for the year's crops. The vegetable garden had to be dug for potatoes; pastures had to be prepared for cattle. This work continued, through second plantings of crops, manuring and hoeing, until early summer. By May or June the bogs were dry enough for turf-cutting. These were also important months for buying and selling livestock, while root crops could be planted as late as mid-June. At the beginning of July lobster inshore fishing was profitable, and for a few communities in the north-west July also marked the beginning of a brief season of drift-netting for salmon.

Haymaking got under way by August, and was closely followed by the harvest of whatever winter feed had been sown – oats in early September, root vegetables in October. At the same time turf had to be carted from the bog and stacked by the house. By mid-September lobster fishing had usually become either too hazardous or too low in yield: pots were stacked and shore nets dried for storage.

May Day, fair season,
perfect is colour then;
blackbirds sing a full lay
if there be a slender beam of day.

Ninth-century Irish poem

Potatoes were harvested in November, although they would be dug for daily use as soon as the 'earlies' ripened in July. After the potato harvest, except for any ploughing or digging the farmer liked to complete before the winter frosts, work on the land was completed. The potato harvest signified in the most real way an end of a season's work: so long as a turf stack stood by the house and the potatoes were dug there would be cooked food for winter and spring. Between December and February was the time for odd jobs about the farm and, more importantly, for talking and dancing and marriage-making.

Of course there were always cows to be milked and clothes to be made and mended, while the children's education had to be kept underway. And the house had to be warmed, the potatoes boiled, the bread baked, the pig fed, the butter churned. ... Many routines did *not* attach to the growing, harvesting, fishing and marketing which dominated the spring and summer months.

But farm work and fishing were for the man. All the other recurrent activities were woman's work. The division of labour between man and woman seemed to lie precisely in the distinction between the seasonal and the continuous. Women milked the cows all year round; men dug the turf in the spring; women saw to the education of the children; men planted the crops. It follows that the winter rest was more or less exclusively a rest for the men. Winter, however, was a time for domesticity, when the men passed much of their time around the home or a neighbour's fire. Although such domesticity could not have lightened the burden of the woman's role, it did draw the families together for whatever festivities took place.

A man could acquire the family land only through inheritance. It was customary for the head of each family to make way before his death for the son who was to take his place. Since it was impossible for a man to find a wife before he was ready for the inheritance, it was essential that parents be ready to accept

*For we are told by a grave Author,** an eminent* French *physician, that* Fish being a prolifick Dyet, *there are more children born in* Roman Catholick Countries *about Nine Months after* Lent, *than at any other season.*

Jonathan Swift: *A Modest Proposal*

[* Rabelais]

retirement. Tenacious as they almost invariably were in their hold on the farm and in their resistance to the inheritor marrying much before he was forty, parents did eventually have to acquiesce to the need for another generation. In relation to the annual cycle, it was inevitable that parents should finally accept change during winter, after the year's harvests were secured and before the arduous early spring work on the land had to be undertaken. The heir's wedding marks his assumption of responsibility for a cycle of work lasting for the most part of a year. Married life for the new householder began with preparing the land to yield another year's subsistence. Further, the bride's dowry had to be settled by her father, and he was best able to calculate it after seeing the year's produce, and most ready to enter long and exacting negotiations when he had time on his hands. It follows that winter was the natural time for giving in to another marriage.

In Connemara today there are many stories retailed poking fun at the unromantic bridegroom. The stories run something like this: driving from the wedding party at his bride's family home to his own new farm, the groom jumps from the trap declaring that his wife should hurry on her way to the home and see to the cows by herself, for he must borrow a plough from the neighbour. Such stories are about the displacement of romantic conceptions by what are taken to be banal preoccupations with work. But it is fair to say that romance for the groom lay precisely in his new status as farmer: collecting a plough from the neighbour is the first act as farmer and householder. And as a farmer he begins in the springtime: seeking out the loan of a plough signifies new status, but it also represents the beginning of the year's work.

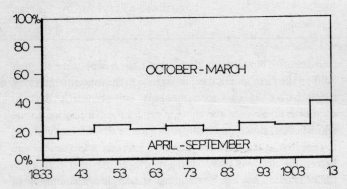

Figure 1. The percentage of marriages occurring in winter and summer for one parish, 1833–1913
Source: Parish records

The table of marriages in Figure 1 shows the remarkable concentration of weddings in the winter months.* These figures are a complete documentation of marriages in one isolated rural parish, and can safely be claimed as representative of rural Ireland over the period 1835–1922.

That marriage was widely regarded as possible only in winter

---

*See *The Sociology of an English Village*, London, 1956, pp. 45 ff. This concentration of marriages in winter has never been a feature of English rural life. W. M. Williams gives the percentage of marriages occurring in each month over a long period for an English rural community:

	J	F	M	A	M	J	Jul	Au	S	O	N	D
1572–1887	9.1	9.0	0.9	7.4	9.0	11.6	8.0	6.9	6.9	7.0	13.9	10.3
1887–1920	8.8	6.9	5.8	0.7	5.5	9.9	6.6	6.0	11.0	10.7	8.2	9.9
1920–1950	7.4	8.0	6.0	12.3	6.0	8.5	6.5	4.4	12.9	13.4	5.4	9.2
1572–1950	9.0	8.2	2.8	8.7	7.6	10.9	7.6	6.7	8.3	8.9	11.5	9.8

is indicated by the phenomenon of 'Skellig lists'. In some parts of County Kerry it was traditional until about thirty years ago for the poets and wits of each village to poke fun in verse at eligible bachelors unwed by the beginning of Lent. These joking rhymes, called 'Skellig lists', recommended marriage on the Skellig Islands. The Skelligs for many centuries contained a monastery carved into their bare rock. When the church calendar was revised the Skellig monks were most resistant to its innovations; long after the rest of Ireland had accepted the revised dating for Holy Days, the Skellig monastery retained the old and traditional religious year. One consequence of the new calendar was the backdating of Lent by a month. In retaining the old calendar, therefore, the monks began and ended Lent one month after anyone on the mainland – or for that matter in the rest of Christendom. This conservatism allowed an extra month for marriage in the main part of winter. The origin of the Skellig list probably lies in this extra month, and the rhymes teased the unwed with the additional chance for a quick match on the Islands, where the monks could perform a ceremony without violating mainland orthodoxy.

The tradition of Skellig lists leaves no doubt as to the rural emphasis on winter marriage. But they also give an indication of the merriment and celebration which accompanied marriage. Once the sub-division of land, which proliferated before the great famine, had been abandoned, it was no longer possible for sons of the peasantry to hasten into early marriages. Further, only one son could inherit, from which it followed that only one son could make a locally important match. The delays and restrictions on marriage which emerged so rapidly in the last half of the nineteenth century added a new importance to each marriage. Alongside these delays and restrictions emerged the matchmaker. Usually an elderly widow, the matchmaker kept her eye open for possible pairings, and acted as go-between or chief negotiator in preliminaries to the deal.

The matchmaker spotted likely couples at dances and parties, the *ceilidhes* which occurred with greater and greater frequency as winter advanced.* She conducted the negotiations through many encounters with all the people involved. She made a point of capturing the young couple's confidences, arranged formal meetings with fathers, and less formally visited the mothers. Visiting made for gossip, and gossip made for matches. Each marriage was preceded by a multitude of dances and fireside discussions, and all the preparations required an endless coming and going between homes. And when the deal was in its final stages the fathers had to endure prolonged and demanding negotiations which in turn required more visiting, while the mothers, family and friends would begin to celebrate the coming marriage with ever-increasing zest.

Each marriage concerned a wide range of people – the widely extended kin as well as neighbours and friends. Probably every villager was involved in every village marriage. There was a sizeable if decreasing number of marriages each winter month

---

The women were over-excited and ... crowded around me and began jeering and shrieking at me because I am not married. A dozen screamed at a time, and so rapidly that I could not understand ... yet I was able to make out that they were taking advantage of the absence of their husbands to give me the full volume of their contempt. Some little boys who were listening threw themselves down writhing with laughter among the seaweed, and the young girls grew red and embarrassed and stared down in the surf.

J. M. Synge quoted in W. B. Yeats: *Synge and
the Ireland of his Time*

---

* The *ceilidhe* (pronounced 'cayly') is the traditional name for Irish country parties. The *ceilidhe* typically took place in a cottage, was open to all the neighbours, and was based on singing, dancing and story-telling.

in the fifty years following the famine.* It is obvious enough
that the winter months – perhaps better called the marriage
months – allowed little respite from a round of parties and
visiting.

To winter festivities surrounding marriages must be added
the Christmas celebrations. It was customary for many farm
families to kill a pig each winter, and to salt down or smoke
whatever part was not eaten fresh for Christmas dinners. But in
the prolonged season of *ceilidhes* Christmas would not have been
the only or most festive day or week. Christmas parties lasted
into the evening, but wedding parties lasted all night and often
enough long into the following day too. Even the least formal
ceilidhes, the ones created by a number of young people agreeing
to meet one night at a particular home in the village, could last
with dancing and singing a whole night through. Perhaps Christmas offered a religious focus to the winter, with rituals of church
rather than party-going.

It has already been pointed out that work in the home did
not cease with the onset of winter. Moreover it is probably an
error to make the same distinction between work and *ceilidhe*

---

*How happy we were waiting for Hallowe'en, and playing the old
Gaelic games – the Ring, the Blind Man, Knucklestones, Trom-
Trom and Hide-and-Seek; a fine red fire sending warmth into
every corner, bright silver sand from the White Strand on the floor
glittering in the lamplight, two boys and two girls going partners at
a game of knucklestones in one corner of the house, four more in
another corner.*

Maurice O'Sullivan: *Twenty Years A-Growing*

---

*From the records of a parish in West Cork the figures for marriages
in January and February alone are: 1850:26; 1860: 19; 1870: 17; 1880:
9; 1890: 8; 1900: 13.

as between work and play in the urban industrial milieu. Much of the winter 'play' in rural Ireland, as we have seen, turned on marriage, and marriage implicated the entire fabric of ownership and responsibility for production. And beyond the issue of marriage is that of mutual aid.

In virtually all peasant societies mutual aid was of critical importance. The full extent and the details of mutual aid in rural Ireland will be described in Chapter 5. But there is an important connection between mutual aid and the intense festivity and visiting of the winter months. The activities associated with marriages involved families in new relationships which would certainly have included a right to call upon one another for help. The advantages of an alliance in terms of mutual aid must have played a good part in the matchmakers' calculations. It follows that winter celebrations also formed and revealed the claims and counter-claims which go to make up a system of aid. Again, the impossibility of making rigid distinctions between work and play is evident. Each part of the year demonstrated the basic continuity of the farm and its family, just as each activity involved the economic basis of the society. Winter festivity and summer work were intimately bound together. In that sense at least winter was not and never could have been the simple absence of work or disregard for the seasonal rounds to come.

During the most intense part of the year's work mutual aid had its overt place. Families paired for the cutting, footing and hauling of turf from the bog, first doing one household's supply and then the other's. Families called upon one another at harvest time and at haymaking, and for thatching of houses, which was in some areas an annual event. Much of this aid was needed by households with very few members, and often a widow could give grazing rather than labour in return for essential help. This last type of aid became more necessary as successive waves of emigration began to depopulate the countryside more extensively, and as more farms came to be occupied by the elderly and the solitary.

One aspect of mutual aid found in almost every society which has developed such a system is the party accompanying the joint work.* When two families worked together at the bog during the day it was customary for the receiving family to entertain the helpers after work – beer or *poteen* would be provided, stories and songs exchanged, and the tea laid on by the hostess for all who had participated in the work. Similarly, the old or isolated person who was receiving the work from neighbours in return for a service like grazing would provide the visiting helpers with a drink or two in the evening, and again the stories would be swapped and a dance or two tried out in the kitchen. At a number of points during the year, therefore, work was mixed with *ceilidhes*, and visiting between houses found another rationale. These were times of the most intense and demanding work, when speed and thoroughness were at their highest premium – haymaking, potato-digging, turf-cutting. The simple opposition of summer work to winter play evidently needs substantial qualification.

The younger people also had their own special summer-time

... *and sitting by the fire one of them cried out, 'Michael Hart, can you tell a story?' 'Never a one,' said I. On that he caught me by the shoulders and put me out like a shot.*

'A Fairy Entertainment' told by
Michael Hart in W. B. Yeats: *Irish Fairy Tales*

---

*The connection between parties or feasts and socio-economic co-operation brings the informal mutual-aid system of Ireland into the same perspective as much more highly structured situations. It is not unrewarding to compare even Kwakiutl Potlach with Irish work *ceilidhes*. For comparable data from another peasant society see J. V. Freitas Marcondes, 'Mutirao or Mutual Aid', *Rural Sociology* 13, 1948, pp. 374–89.

Danny: *Down where the bees are humming ...*
Barry: *But when the light is soft 'n dim,*
discovery disarming,
The modest moon behind the clouds, young
maidens, coy 'n charming,
Still cuddle men who cuddle them, 'n carry
on alarming,
Danny: *Down where the bees are humming an' the*
wild flowers gaily growing.

Sean O'Casey: *The End of the Beginning*

---

activities, and of these the most striking was the crossroads dancing. On fine evenings the young men and women of the parish would gather at a crossroads, and there to the accompaniment of fiddle or accordion or even simply to the lilting of those standing out they would dance through the long twilights of midsummer.

It is said that in many country districts these dances were occasion for much flirtation, and as the dark came down on the dancers couples would often be seen edging their way from the main crowd, and would be noticed by their families coming home long after nightfall. It seems that the families themselves were inclined to indulge such flirtations, but there are many stories told of priests in the countryside who did not. These priests used to walk the country lanes after dark, striking at the hedgerows with their sticks, seeking out and roundly belabouring the erring young disturbed in their secret hideouts by the roadside. It is also told that many priests used their midsummer sermons to inveigh against this disrespect for Christian teachings. These tales most surely indicate the use to which the crossroads dance was put, when the long summer evenings offered a chance to the young for their parties after work.

The older people had a tradition of their own called night-walking. Each evening after the day's work, when there was nothing more formal already arranged, an old man walked to a neighbour's house to make an impromptu visit. Often, of course, the neighbour had done the same thing himself, and so the first walker would continue on to another house. In this way people gathered, and sat exchanging stories and discussing the progress of the season. Although most country people of the west today remember these walks as quite unplanned, there are parts of northern Donegal where a house was chosen each night for the *ceilidhe*; all who had anything they wished to discuss went inside, while the younger people sang and danced outside.* No doubt the practice varied a great deal from one part of the countryside to another, but one thing is sure; visiting, talking and entertainments did not cease, as the marriages did, with the start of a year's work on the land.

The activities of all seasons, including winter, were part of a single social and economic whole. Preoccupation with the farm persisted through fireside chats and matchmaking of winter just as it lay behind night-walking. Amusements untainted with conscious economic interest were perhaps the province of the young at crossroads dances or of the couples dodging detection along country lanes after dark. And just as the Irish country people rarely lost sight of farm and the subsistence on which their life was based, neither did they abandon under a summer sun their love of dancing and singing and story-telling. The

---

Geancanach (*ghan-can-ak*): *A fairy who smokes a pipe and loves milkmaids. Applied to anyone who is constantly talking of his amours: if a man loses money because of women it is said he must have met a* geancanach.

Dictionary of Irish Mythology

---

* This is described by Patrick Gallagher: see *Paddy the Cope: My Story*, Jonathan Cape, 1939.

seasons determined the settings and in some measure the social forms of all these activities. The activities themselves were not simply a consequence of name of month or time of year. The community came together most completely for all the winter festivities, whereas the clusters of farms and the groups of villagers implicated in the debt and credit of mutual aid came together in summer. At no time did the community scatter each into his individual home: it was against a background of community, with a consciousness of community, that the year's activities, summer and winter, all took place.

It is in relation to this traditionally resilient and enduring community life that the drastic changes which have occurred in the past three decades must be seen. Today there are very real oppositions between summer and winter. But the most important single feature of the opposition is precisely the one which derives from the atrophy and disappearance of community. Now there is a time of year – indeed, the substantial part of the year – when community life is absolutely minimal. Now it *is* possible to talk of the opposition between summer and winter in terms of the absence or residual presence of that community. The difference between rural Ireland today and the traditional situation is largely to do with the difference between a society where the community is strong and enduring and one where community life is weak and intermittent. Among the many other changes and reversals that have taken place in the Irish country-side, this emergence of an opposition between different times of the year is of the most fundamental importance. The atrophy and finally the eclipse of communal activity and mutual inter-dependence are, for a small rural community, the onset of certain demoralization. Social upheavals and changes which occur in such a context will invariably reflect a resurgence of the communality which is in decline. The absence of such movements in rural Ireland indicates the completeness of the de-moralization.

*Connor, be it known, would drink a quart of salt water, for its
medicinal virtues, before breakfast; and for the same reason, I
suppose, double that quantity of raw whisky between breakfast and
night, which last he did with as little inconvenience to himself as
any man in the barony of Mogferton.*

'Flory Contillon's Funeral' in W. B. Yeats (ed.):
Fairy and Folk Tales

Innumerable writers have described the Irishman's heavy
drinking. Synge wrote in 1905 of a boat's perilous crossing from
Dingle to the Great Blasket manned by the fiercely drunk
returning from a mainland fair.* Distilling *poteen* in the rural
districts according to K. H. Connell, was an alternative in the
domestic economy to churning butter for sale.† And no doubt
a fair measure of that 'mountain dew' was consumed on the
still-owner's farm. In the countryside today the older men
celebrate with many tales the great good use they made of
whisky which was once obtainable, in the folk memory at least,
for next to nothing a keg. Certainly these accounts and memories
of past drinking have some connection with the observable
drinking habits of today. What cannot be observed, however, is
the increase or decrease in rural insobriety. Tourists to the
villages of the western seaboard are likely to be struck by a quite
remorseless consumption of porter and whisky. In the village
bars, from early evening to the late closing time, there is a crowd
of regulars – the same men taking ten or a dozen pints of
Guinness chased by a few measures of Irish in a manner sug-
gestive of a well-formed habit.

But the tourist will also observe that this volume of drink is
taken with great enjoyment, and the drunkenness it precipitates

*J. M. Synge, *In Wicklow and West Kerry*, Dublin, 1912, p. 45.
†See K. H. Connell's essay on illicit distillation in *Irish Peasant
Society* (Oxford University Press, 1968), pp. 1–51.

is full of laughter: the men in the bars are outgoing, excited, welcoming to stranger and neighbour alike. On a Saturday dance night the occasional brawl erupts in bars adjacent to the village hall, but these are not serious fights, and in any case are usually caused by aggressive young men home from the cities for the summer visit to their families who have travelled to the dance from a relatively distant parish. Among the local men, the tourist will see above all a cheerfulness and goodwill in all stages of the drinking. Far more than either the changes in consumption over the years or the sheer volume of alcohol at present consumed by many villagers of the west, it is the form assumed by drunkenness itself which yields most insight. Most important of all, drunken behaviour varies with the time of year. Improbable as this may at first sound, these are among the most important clues to changes which the traditional annual cycle has sustained.

The drunkenness in which the tourist participates occurs during the brief summer holiday season. It is a drunkenness of elation and extroversion. In the winter months, however, this elation gives way to its opposite. The men in the bars during the summer talk fast and loud. In the winter the same men talk – when they talk at all – slowly and quietly. As they drink in the winter months they appear depressed and withdrawn.

Most winter evenings a few men gather in each bar. The very manner in which they walk into the bar often suggests a curiously subdued state of mind. The newcomer greets those already at the bar, asks for his drink, and falls silent. Conversational exchanges between drinkers are abrupt and cursory. There is rarely any ongoing dialogue. Pauses between the few fragments of dialogue are long. Each speaker hesitates so much for thought, and anticipates so little by way of response or reply, that his few words are often left suspended in the bar's quiet too long for the next words to sound like a reply. Indeed, the most frequent real reply is simple accord, the familiar 'Ah, 'tis'.

These men do not stay for the long hours in the bars which

characterize their summer drinking nor do they often consume the sheer volume of alcohol drunk in summer.* But when they do drink hard and the effects of the drinking begin to appear, despondency becomes more extreme and its behavioural indices more overt. A drunken man in winter leans more heavily on the bar. He often seeks to draw another drinker or two to his side. Such a group creates a tight circle of privacy around itself – a privacy physically expressed by the arms they lay across one another's shoulders. Then, with faces almost touching, they appear to join closely in evident despair. This despair is not expressed in discussion among the drinkers. Rather, they exchange silence as if it were words, and words in brief expressions of the lonesomeness.

The mood of these groups is close to that of some of the more nostalgic songs which the same people so conspicuously enjoy on summer evenings. And it is a mood which conveys the bar's atmosphere, perhaps with only one man leaning there slowly taking his pint in complete silence. The single customer will often exchange but the scarcest and most peremptory words with the bartender. Often such a solitary figure goes into a bar night after night, spends an hour over a pint or two, maintaining all the time an air of intense absorption, and leaves after speaking perhaps fewer than a dozen words. On Sundays after mass, when a good crowd fills the bars, its ease, whatever the time of year, is helped by a sense of the parish community around the church. But even then the winter crowd is quieter, its drinking less hectic, its conviviality subdued.

Just as the opposite forms which drinking and drunkenness assume indicate the radical difference between summer and

* In winter there is usually less money in the villages: migrants tend to bring their 'roll' in summer, and there are fewer markets in winter. But money does not dry up altogether, while a shortage of cash certainly explains neither the different behaviour in the bar nor the distinctive winter drunkenness.

winter moods, so the part played by singing in the bars indicates both how precious and how brief is the summer elation. In many bars, most particularly in the remoter rural districts, it is singing which dominates the summer evenings. Everyone known to be a singer – in many areas amounting to a sizeable proportion of the community – is cajoled and encouraged into giving an unaccompanied rendering of a song for which he is known. Tourists are also asked for a song, and if someone carries a guitar he is encouraged to play accompaniment. In many cases, however, the majority if not all of the performers are local men. But very little singing is heard outside the tourist season. On one occasion one of the best known singers of a small village in West Cork declared to me that he could not bring himself to sing any song at all before the first of July.

It is only after the beginning of July that a large number of tourists begins to arrive in the remoter seaboard villages. Very few remain after mid-September. At the most there are ten weeks of the year when strangers and outsiders play any significant role in the daily social life of the community. Further, the tourist period also coincides with the time when migrants return for a holiday or lobster fishing or to help with the farm work at haymaking and harvest time.

The year can now be characterized as elation in summer and despondency for the rest of the year. Traditionally it was marriages which provided the focus for the most intense social activity in winter. Figure 2 shows how the number of marriages has declined in one parish in the last fifty years. With so few marriages there is correspondingly less winter festivity; but decline in the number of marriages has been accompanied by another important change. The comparatively small number of couples who do marry in the west of Ireland have come to prefer a summer marriage. Figure 3 shows the extent to which marriages have become concentrated in the summer months. Since winter marriage was urged by the demands of traditional farm

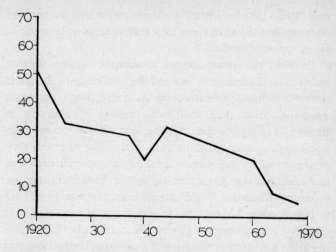

Figure 2. The number of marriages occurring in one parish, 1920–1968
Source: Parish records

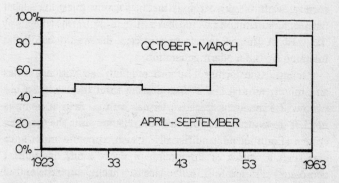

Figure 3. The percentage of marriages occurring in winter and summer for one parish, 1923–63
Source: Parish records

and family life, it follows from the preference for summer marriage that those demands have either ceased to be made or are no longer accepted.

In either case these changes in marriage customs indicate the decline of community life and the weakening of the social system which was nourished by it. Young people dissociate themselves from their traditional heritage by marrying in summer, and signify their involvement with an entirely different kind of society by the kind of wedding reception they prefer. It used to be customary for a couple to return from church to the bride's home for the wedding *ceilidhe*. Usually a neighbour of the bride's family would complete the preparation of food and drink while the ceremony took place and the *ceilidhe* began directly the couple returned from church. After the celebrations the bride was taken to the groom's new farm. Today, however, the couple go from church directly to the smartest hotel the bride's family has been able to find, for a more 'modern' reception. They hire cars to take the guests, and all food is provided by the hoteliers. The *ceilidhe* is eliminated. This summer marriage is accompanied by the symbols of a very different society. With the girls strongly inclined against marrying a local farmer, a matchmaker would have little to do in the villages of the west of Ireland today; in any case she would hardly be tolerated by the modern generation.

Alongside the decline of interest and faith in traditional values and mores, mutual aid is disappearing from the land. An old widow or a mentally defective farmer with no help at home is not left destitute by neighbours and relatives, but the complex system of mutual aid, traditionally of such economic importance and such a source of interaction of every kind, has almost completely disappeared. In its place is a strong emphasis on the privacy and self-reliance of each household. The erosion of mutual aid has made way for an ethic of independence. The consequences for the seasonal round are quite drastic. Instead

Decline in neighbourliness reflects the growing individualism of the family. The common adage 'have it yourself or leave it after you' indicates the accepted attitude to neighbours. Both men and women said they rarely visited neighbours except on business, and it was surprising the number of people who had never been inside the homes of their immediate neighbours.

Limerick Rural Survey

of a winter of intense sociability matched by a summer of work which turned on myriad forms of interdependence, there exists today a long and rarely interrupted quiet. Night-walking exists only residually; crossroads dances have not been seen in more than a decade; Skellig lists are a thing of the past. Just as the drinkers outside the tourist season seem silenced by the very weather and stay hunched and withdrawn at the bar, the separate farm families withdraw for the winter into themselves. Christmas is now a subdued holiday, and the few migrants who return from the cities of Ireland and England complain about the lack of life they find at home.

St Brigid's Day marks today, as it did a hundred years ago, the beginning of work on the land. The land still must be turned and made ready for potatoes; pastures for the cattle must be attended to. Spring still brings the fine drying weather which sends men onto the bogs to cut the turf, and a few fishermen shoot their inshore lobster pots each calm day between July and September. Seine-netting for herring and mackerel has ceased to be important: the herring appear to have shifted their routes away from the coves and estuaries of the western seaboard; the markets for salted mackerel have long since collapsed. Yet the turf must be hauled in late summer, and cattle must be taken to market at the local fairs. Work on the land must continue, cultivation of subsistence foodstuffs and marketable produce is still integral to the farm economy. But there is a critical

> The world looks on
> And talks of the peasant:
> The peasant has no worries;
> In his little lyrical fields
> He ploughs and sows.
> ...
> The travellers stop their cars to gape over the
> green bank into his fields
> ...
> The travellers touch the root of the grave and
> feel reassured
> When they grasp the steering wheels again.
>
> Patrick Kavanagh: *The Great Hunger*

difference between the former communalization and the present privatization of work. Today's farmers work by themselves for themselves.

Only with the presence of the tourists for a few summer weeks is the prolonged withdrawal and quiet of the Irish countryside much interrupted. What tourists bring each year are numbers, girls, money and reassurance. It is the last of these which is the most important.

It is tempting to regard sheer additional numbers as the magic ingredient by which tourists turn a silent and withdrawn bar into a centre of vivacity and extroversion. The countryside has been suffering depopulation for over a century. In many parts of the western regions of Ireland the population has become extremely sparse. Where once there stood a cluster of a dozen houses there often remains but one or two. It follows from this that the distance between farm families has become greater and the sheer difficulty of visiting bar and neighbour may inhibit much social interaction. To some extent the traditional communality may have depended upon proximity.

Hence the small numbers in the bars, and hence the quiet. With the addition of tourists the numbers are swollen enough to prevent the possibility of that quiet. Hence the impression of a sudden resurgence of community. The objections to that argument, however, are substantial. During the tourist season far more local people go to the bars far more often. Even when there are only three or four tourists in a bar to fifteen or twenty local people, the local people are full of talk and celebration. Further, during the tourist season drunkenness gives rise to talk, song and joy whether tourists are 'making the crowd' or not. It may be the case that tourists attract a crowd; it is not the case that the crowd or its mood are dominated by their numbers.

The presence of tourist girls in the communities during the summer is another possible key to the difference between summer and the rest of the year. Girls have emigrated in greater numbers than men from every part of the countryside; the disproportionate number of bachelors in the remoter communities is one of their most striking features. The majority of the men in the bars are usually bachelors between twenty and fifty. It is they who dominate the bars' moods and they are the ones most likely to be responsive to the presence of girls and women among the tourists – girls and women who do frequent the bars and do participate, unlike local women, in the nightly rounds of drinking, talking and singing. Yet it is striking how few of these bachelors try to make any contact with the tourist women beyond occasional chatter. They are, for the most part, nervous of women and become embarrassed very quickly by encounters with them. It is extremely rare to hear of any sexual intimacy between tourist and local bachelor. Moreover, even when the tourists are all men the spirited evenings still occur.

In the same way, even where the tourists are not bringing much money with them, they still seem to inject zest and enthusiasm into the community. And the people who exhibit the most zest are the ones who benefit financially the least, and

'Bedad, then,' he said, 'isn't it a great wonder that you've seen France, and Germany, and the Holy Father, and never seen a man making kelp till you came to Inishmaan.'

An Aran islander, quoted in
J. M. Synge: *The Aran Islands*

are also the ones who behave with the greatest and surest generosity towards visitors, buying drinks and inviting them home for tea and more drinks.

What the tourists do most surely bring to these communities, however, is reassurance and approval. The erosion of traditional sociability is intimately connected with erosion of the country-man's faith and belief in his society. Society in the countryside has declined alongside the contraction of farming activity. Very few farms are larger than they need be to secure the minimum of provision and income. Decline in population has made a larger farm difficult to run, and on many farms remittances have made it possible to survive with a low level of activity on the land and sea. But alongside this social atrophy and economic contraction there has developed a striking lack of conviction about the advantage, merit or desirability of living and working in a small rural community. Traditional life is valued defensively where it is valued at all. And that defensiveness takes the form: it's good to have a bit of quiet and fresh air the fine months of the year. Remaining on the land for many of the local people is tantamount to accepting a limited, restrictive, inadequate life.

In many small but significant ways Irish country people indicate symbolically their involvement with the urban culture to which they are tending to look for social and moral guidance. Young men wear the clothes they think would impress an urban visitor. The housewife places great emphasis on tidiness and cleanliness in the home. The father accepts the son's entitlement

In hotels and bars, in Youghal, Caherciveen, Donaghadee, Tallaght, Camden Town, Inisheen, and Kilburn – in any place where our people have gathered – I have bested them all. If someone said he had been to Texas, and hunted cattle, I was hot on his heels with my story of a weekend spent with a sheik in East Tunis.
Brendan Behan: *Tell Me Another*

to independence. Young girls are preoccupied with the latest Dublin and London fashions. In conversation with tourists, villagers tend to emphasize their awareness of rural limitations and seem to hope that they can establish their superiority to traditional life. In the homes, the stranger is offered white bread and shop ham on the assumption that these are bound to be preferred to rugged home produce, and in the hope of showing the visitor that even if they, the hosts, are Irish country people they still know what is really good. In these anticipations and symbolic gestures – some of them astute, others naïve – the country people seek to demonstrate their esteem for urban life. By the same token they indicate their profound dissatisfaction with local and national tradition.

What the tourists do, however, is to affirm *their* esteem for the rural milieu and its ways. By travelling to a remote parish the tourists indicate approval for it.* And when they are staying, it is singing and conviviality in the bar, the fishing and the scenery itself, which they are both explicitly and implicitly complimenting. The presence of these outsiders, these representatives of the social and cultural forms which the country people so frequently unquestioningly assume to be superior to

* Often this approval is not taken for granted. That local people are often unsatisfied by a show of mere interest is indicated by their anxious questioning of the tourist – questioning which aims at defining the approval. In this respect tourists can be compared to an audience which the actors are never sure of. I return to this in Chapter 6.

---

*I came to understand how much knowledge of the real life of
Ireland went to the creation of a world which is yet as fantastic as
the Spain of Cervantes. Here is the story of* The Playboy, *and*
The Shadow of the Glen; *here is the ghost on horseback ...
numberless ways of speech and vehement pictures that had seemed to
owe nothing to observation, and all to some overflowing of himself.*

W. B. Yeats: *Synge and the Ireland of his Time*

---

their own, thus gives a renewed confidence in their own society
and culture.

The bachelors of the communities are potentially the most
depressed group, and certainly are the people most directly
disadvantaged by any comparison between the life style of the
urban bachelor and their own. Many of these men have accepted
their life in duty to ageing parents' wishes rather than in any
enthusiasm for the kind of life entailed in remaining on the land.
It is this group of men who most conspicuously accept a minimal
farm and who can see little future in the life they have been
obliged by circumstances to endure. The withdrawal and the
depression of the winter period is very much a function of this
group's predominance and social importance. They are the men
who, in frequenting the bars, have assumed a public significance
even beyond their social importance. And in frequenting the
bars, this is the group which comes most certainly into contact
with the summer tourist. That contact gives them the approval
which their sense of relative disadvantage denies.

The traditional seasonal round of work has not disappeared –
much of the work on the land is still the same. But the quality of
life in rural Ireland today is indicated by the atrophy of the
social quality which formerly imbued almost every part of the
year's activity. Instead there has evolved a radical opposition
between the short tourist season and the principal mood of the
rest of the year.

In suggesting that the quality of social life is a key to understanding the contemporary situation and a means of approaching
the most important social changes, a move is made from a
behavioural to a perceptual level of description. It is what
people feel – their moods and attitudes – which provides the
basis of the account instead of what they are doing. There is no
evidence to suggest that the moods and attitudes of people in
rural Ireland in the traditional society varied particularly from
season to season. More important, there is no evidence for saying
that traditionally the countryside suffered from the despondency
and pessimism which are so apparent today. It is the prevalence
of this despondency which strikes a visitor to the western districts
of Ireland during the quiet of the year. It is a despondency which
is at once distressing and puzzling. It is the feature of country
life most strikingly at odds with so much of what is said and
written of the past.

In the following chapters the circumstances – historical,
social and economic – which lie behind this human demoralization will be described. The state of mind which dominates the
large part of the year today attaches to a number of striking
sociological factors. In relation to the traditional year it was

---

April, and no one able to calculate
How far it is to harvest. They put down
The seeds blindly with sensuous groping fingers,
And sensual sleep dreams subtly underground.
Tomorrow is Wednesday – who cares?
'Remember Eileen Farrelly? I was thinking
A man might do a damned sight worse....' That
              voice is blown
Through a hole in a garden wall –
And who was Eileen now cannot be known.
                    Patrick Kavanagh: *The Great Hunger*

---

possible to grasp the connections between the socio-economic structures and the fabric of entertainments and festivity at each season and according to each material need. In the present situation, on the other hand, the connections have changed. The apparent persistence of an economic form – the farming and fishing, the blend of subsistence and marketing – is deceptive. In truth, the entire fabric of country life of the vast majority of communities in the west of Ireland has drastically altered. It remains for the rest of this book to follow each of those changes in its forms and consequences.

I have long felt the inconvenience resulting from the ignorance of the English people generally, of the history of Ireland. Why should they not be ignorant of that history? The story itself is full of no other interest than a painful one, disgusting from its details of barbarous infliction on the one hand, and partial and therefore driftless resistance on the other. To the English it seems enough to know, that one way or the other Ireland had become subject to England.

William Cobbett: *A History of the Protestant Reformation*

In virtually every part of the west of Ireland conditions are inimical to highly productive or intensive farming. Top soil is thin, infertile and rocky. The abundance of stone walls enclosing the smallest pastures and garden plots gives an indication of how great was the volume of rock cleared from every acre of land. There are huge tracts of soft bog, only the edges of which could be painstakingly drained and fertilized enough for a crop. And the land has been stripped of its trees, leaving the ground with only meagre protection against wind and water erosion. Even the bare grasslands of the west are sited in steeply undulating countryside. The shoreline is rugged and dangerous, offering little shelter or harbouring and leaving fishermen unnervingly exposed to the sudden violence of Atlantic storms. As a region, the west of Ireland is hardly suitable for either farming

I have seen nothing so desolate. Grey floods of water were sweeping everywhere upon the limestone, making at times a wild torrent of the road, which twined continually over low hills and cavities in the rock or passed between a few small fields of potatoes or grass hidden away in corners that had shelter.

J. M. Synge: *The Aran Islands*

It is a country where the bones of the earth stick through its starved skin.

George Russell, describing the Rosses region of Donegal

or fishing. For at least three hundred years this land supported a large and resilient peasantry – a peasantry concentrated in its densest population at the very western edges of the island.

The history of this peasantry is extraordinary for the changes and disruptions which it survived. The more distant background of the communities which remain today in this conspicuously unfavourable environment lies in centuries of invasion, destruction and recovery – each following the other in a cycle familiar only to societies made the object of remorseless and protracted exploitation.* The colonization of Ireland was believed to have been secured by the close of the reign of Henry VIII. Behind that belief lay appalling devastation of the countryside. Similar devastation periodically accompanied reassertion of English hegemony in Ireland under Elizabeth I and Cromwell.

It must never be forgotten that the British determination to colonize stemmed from a belief that in Ireland lay an extremely rich and desirable territory. Simple greed for the country's

* See George A. T. O'Brien, *The Economic History of Ireland in the Seventeenth Century*, Dublin, 1919. He takes the cycle of devastation and recovery as his introductory thesis. See also J. C. Beckett, *A Short History of Ireland*, London, 1952, who documents the Elizabethan determination to anglicize Gaelic society.

fruitfulness was of course reinforced and complicated by a more directly political feeling that an Ireland hostile or in the empire of an enemy would leave England vulnerable. The glories of Ireland as a source of wealth and fighting men were for a millennium an important part of European consciousness. In the ninth century St Donatus, then Bishop of Etruria, wrote a poem on the theme. Printed here in an eighteenth-century translation it gives lyrical expression to the myth of wealth, to be won in Ireland:

> Far westward lies an isle of ancient fame,
> By nature bless'd, and Scotia* is her name;
> An island rich – exhaustless is her store
> Of veiny silver and of golden ore;
> Her fruitful soil forever teems with wealth,
> With gems her waters, and her air with health.
>
> Her verdant fields with milk and honey flow,
> Her woolly fleeces vie with virgin snow;
> Her waving furrows float with bearded corn
> And arms and arts her envy'd sons adorn.
> No savage bear with lawless fury roves,
> No rav'ning lion through her sacred groves,
> No poison there infects, no scaly snake
> Creeps through the grass, nor frog annoys the lake.

This view of the country's riches endured into the seventeenth century. At the period of most directly political justification for invasion, colonization and anglicization, the material incentives for the enterprise were not forgotten. In a letter of 1612 Bacon noted that Ireland was

endowed with so many dowries of nature, considering the fruitfulness of the soil, the ports, the rivers, the fishings, the quarries, the

* The Scoti were a group of people who lived in Ireland and migrated to Scotland in the fifth century, hence the ambiguous use of 'Scotia'.

woods, and other materials, and especially the race and generation of men, valiant, hard and active, as it is not easy, no not upon the Continent, to find such confluence of commodities, if the hand of man did join with the hand of nature.*

Yet the centuries preceding the great famine of 1846–51, although basic to the political history of Ireland and notorious for devastation, are surprisingly distant from subsequent developments. The early movements of population (which included substantial emigration) were mostly confined to Protestants who feared that the Catholic Irish were going to succeed militarily in Ireland; equally, the re-allocation of land, so disruptive to Gaelic landowners, did not greatly affect the peasantry.† The Cromwellian settlement certainly did not create a Protestant society. Rather by stripping Catholics of their wealth and excluding them from political institutions, it helped to establish a Protestant ruling class. Thus the social base, the centre of Gaelic culture, was able to endure with a continuity unavailable to any other social group.‡ The peasantry were less

* Quoted by I. Edward Nojan, *The Irish People (Their Height, Form and Strength)*, Dublin, 1899, p. 18.

† As early as the fifteenth century Irish migration to England was established. 'Irish beggars plagued the English populace continually despite a series of enactments following that of 1413 designed to void them out of the realm. The Irish seasonal harvester was already a familiar summer visitor early in the eighteenth century and small colonies of Irish were apparent in most of the major cities' (John A. Jackson, 'The Irish in Britain', *Sociological Review*, 10, 1962, p. 56). This movement almost certainly implicated the population along the east coast of Ireland.

‡ Of course this was not the case in Ulster, where both transference of land to Scottish Protestants and the organized displacement of Catholic Irish were on a massive scale. In Ulster, a Protestant community was created. Ironically enough, its creation was a direct English response to the most effective resistance by Ulster Gaelic lords and the Catholic peasantry to English domination.

That Robert Wallace, being arraigned of the death of John, the son of Juror MacGillemony, by him feloniously slain, and so forth, came and well acknowledged that he slew the aforesaid John, yet he said, that by his slaying he could not commit felony, because he said, that the aforesaid John was a mere Irishman.

Plea of the Crown before the Lord Justice
in Waterford, 1310

damaged than their traditional lords. Indeed, the establishment of an alien upper class with a foreign language, a rival religion and quite distinctive social mores, gave definition to the Irish cultural heritage, and provided at least initially a profound source of solidarity and determination to preserve and perpetuate it, while the British resolve to keep Ireland economically weak maintained the isolation of the peasantry. English governments were still preoccupied with the anglicization both by language and religion of the rural Irish in the middle of the nineteenth century. This testifies to the peasants' comparative invulnerability to upheavals which entirely eclipsed the Gaelic ruling classes. 'The tempest that devastated the castle swept over the cabin' is a particularly apposite comment on rural Ireland before 1847.

By the eighteenth century Gaelic society was the society of the peasantry, most particularly the peasantry living in the poorer, least fertile regions. During the century this society underwent two momentous and interdependent changes: the population, on the more conservative estimates, doubled; the land under cultivation was drastically subdivided. These changes completed the process by which the most people were crowded onto the worst land.

The productivity of the land in Ireland increased with the extensive use of the potato. The great advantage of the potato to Irish agriculture lies in its suitability to wet, rocky and boggy

The other day the man of this house made a new field. ... The old man and his eldest son dug out the clay, with the care of men working a gold-mine, and Michael packed it in panniers ... for transport to a flat rock in a sheltered corner of the holding, where it was mixed with sand and seaweed and spread out in a layer upon the shore.

J. M. Synge: *The Aran Islands*

land. Potatoes can be grown in 'lazy-beds' – rows of earth piled into regular mounds with seaweed or sods as a fertile and substantial base – which allow a crop in the poorest land in the wettest regions. Further, lazy-beds can be worked on steep hillsides in shallow top soil, in ground where no plough could ever be used. A commentator writing in 1816 noted that soft bogs as well as steep braes are inaccessible to the plough, as is rocky ground; 'but a potato crop with a trifling addition to expense can be had from all these, and after the second crop the soil is so completely mellowed, the grain can be put in by spade alone, with a little labour'. As the use of the potato became more and more widespread during the eighteenth century, so the land became able to support more and more people. Also, since enough potatoes for one family could be grown from a relatively small acreage, the number of families could also increase. But for the number of families to increase, land had to be divided – fathers had to allot portions of their farms to sons when the sons wished to marry.

Sub-division was not caused by the new use of the potato. Rather, the usefulness of the potato consisted precisely in its facilitating sub-division. A number of quite different factors urged sub-division on the peasantry. By sub-dividing his land the tenant could divide the rent, and even if the sum of rent payable increased, individual shares could be substantially reduced; the disappearance of the rundale system, and the letting of land in conacre* aggravated the tendency; the sharing of the land between sons solved the problems of the disinherited, and helped families to stay together. The result of these factors was willingness to sub-divide. This sub-division allowed early marriages, which in turn tended to increase the population, inducing further sub-division.

K. H. Connell, who explains in this way the dramatic increase in Irish population between 1750 and 1845, shows how these forces

finally resulted in the grazing being divided into units smaller than the cow's grass or 'sum', such as the 'foot', a quarter cow's grass, and even the 'cleet', which was half a 'foot'. The confusion in the dispersed tillage holdings as a result of sub-division almost defied attempts to carry on; an example is quoted of a half-acre field held by twenty-six different people.†

E. E. Evans remarks on the same feature of Irish eighteenth-century and early nineteenth-century life, noting 'cases on record where 29 partnership-peasants shared 422 plots of ground, where one man held 32 different patches'.‡ This sub-division and the large population it promoted was made possible by the potato. Families lived on potatoes and milk, which, eaten in sufficient quantities, secure adequate health and apparently in

*Rundale was the joint ownership and use of land by an entire community; conacre was the letting of land which had already been prepared for a crop.

†K. H. Connell's argument has been challenged by Michael Drake who suggests that the food value of the potato increased fecundity and reduced infant mortality, and that Connell's account of early marriage is substantially based on incautious interpretation of too literary data. See Michael Drake, 'Marriage and Population Growth in Ireland, 1710–1845', *Economic History Review*, 2nd series, XVI, 2, 1963, pp. 307–13. I am not able to judge between the two historians but neither deny that between 1750 and 1850 the age of men at marriage did decrease and that sub-division proliferated.

‡E. Estyn Evans, *Irish Heritage*, Dundalk, 1949, p. 51.

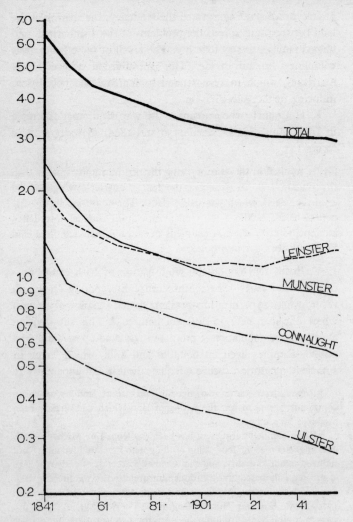

Figure 4. Population of Ireland and Irish provinces, 1841–1951
(ratio scale)
Source: Irish Census, 1956

no way impede fertility. The population of Ireland is not easily estimated for any time before 1800, but after that approximate figures can be agreed:

1603:   750,000

1672: 1,100,000

1801: 5,000,000

1821: 6,000,000

1831: 7,700,000

1841: 8,175,000

Figure 4 gives the overall subsequent population decline for each region of the country.

On the eve of the great famine, therefore, the peasantry of Ireland were dependent upon the potato for their subsistence. The countryside of the remotest and least fertile regions supported huge numbers of families, none of which could have endured without the potato, and few of which held sufficient or adequate lands for any other crop. It is thought that peasants ate between ten and fourteen pounds of boiled potatoes per day. This was an adequate diet, as is shown in Table 1.

Before considering the changes which the famine brought to the Irish peasantry, it must be noted that despite the large increase in population and sub-division, emigration was surprisingly high for the first part of the nineteenth century. Indeed emigration had been a part of Irish life since the Tudor invasion and the internecine strife which accompanied the English conquests of the following three hundred years. But the earlier emigrations were religious and political. Migrations among the peasantry of the western regions are reflected in the higher figures which begin around 1800. The emigration between 1770 and 1815 has been estimated at 4,000 per year, whereas between 1815 and 1845 a total of 1,000,000 emigrated to America alone: an annual average of more than 30,000.*

* Census returns give intercensal emigration figures in numbers and percentages. Virtually every writer on Ireland reviews the earlier

Table 1: Food Value in the Traditional Irish Diet

	calories	protein gm	calcium gm	iron mgm	vit. A international units	thiamin (vit. B1) mgm	riboflavin (vit. G) mgm	niacin (nicotinic acid) mgm	ascorbic acid (vit. C) mgm	Vit. D international units
Recommended by Food and Nutrition Board of National Research Council, U.S.A.	3,000	70	0·56	8·4	3,500	1·26	1·89	12·6	52·5	280 (not including supplement from sunshine)
per 10 lb boiled potatoes*	3,459	45	1·92	21·34	1,600	5·76	0·36–0·48	22·67	444–1,218	0
per pint fresh whole milk	393	19	0·71	0·41	797–3,983	39·3	0·59–1·77	?	171–1,650	winter: 171–389 summer: 1,366–2,162
per 10 lb boiled plus 1 pint milk	3,852	64	2·63	21·75	3,990	45·06	1·60	22·67 + ?	1,741	280–1,764 (winter and summer averages)

*K. H. Connell's figures are for potatoes boiled for thirty minutes and peeled before cooking. The Irish did not peel their potatoes before boiling, and so there was considerably less loss of food value.

Source: K. H. Connell, *The Population of Ireland, 1750–1845*, Oxford University Press, 1950.

To see Ireland happy you must carefully select your point of view,
look for some narrow, isolated spot, and shut your eyes to all the
objects that surround it; but wretched Ireland, on the contrary,
bursts upon your view everywhere.

A French visitor to Ireland in the 1830s, quoted in
R. B. McDowell (ed.): *Social Life in Ireland*, 1805–1845

It was supposed by English politicians and travellers alike at
this time that no population would be willing to endure the
low standards of living and material circumstances which
dominated rural Ireland. But this view reflected a number of
misapprehensions. It derived from ignorance of how the poor
throughout Europe, both peasant and worker, had in fact lived
for centuries. It involved a failure to appreciate how the
peasantry, exactly because they were many and poor, led a life
of complex mutual interdependence. And it resulted from a lack
of appreciation of how the tenant-landlord system tended to
emphasize the *appearance* of destitution: where a tenant appeared
prosperous a landlord came to expect higher rents. The un-
willingness to emigrate, while surprising those few English who
concerned themselves with the plight of rural Ireland, in fact
reflected a number of most important realities in Irish life. It
also reflected, of course, the measure in which emigration of
former years had only marginally implicated the remoter districts
in the belief that there existed in emigration a route to a better
and more exciting life. The realities in fact are perhaps better
called protections. The socio-economic system created by pre-
famine conditions involved a disaffection for emigration which

emigration figures. See for example J. C. Beckett, op. cit.; F. H. A.
Aalen, 'A Review of Recent Irish Population Trends', *Population
Studies*, 17, 1963–4, pp. 73–99; George A. T. O'Brien (ed.), *The
Vanishing Irish*, London: Allen, 1954; T. W. Freeman, *Pre-Famine
Ireland*, Manchester University Press, 1957.

may have been changing a little before the famine, but was only revised on a substantial scale with the famine itself.*

It is scarcely possible to exaggerate in imagination what people will and are forced to do before they die from absolute want of food, for not only does the body become darkened, the feelings callous, blunted and apathetic, but a peculiar fever was generated.... In this state of what may almost be called mania, before the final collapse takes place, the victim sinks into utter prostration through inanition.... Thus a stipendiary magistrate stated in Galway in extenuation of the crime of a poor prisoner brought up for stealing food, that to his own knowledge ... he and his family had actually consumed part of a human body lying dead in the cabin with them ... the actually starving people lived on the carcasses of diseased cattle, upon dogs and dead horses, but principally upon the herbs of the field, nettle tops, wild mustard, and water cresses, and even in some places dead bodies were found with grasses in their mouths.

Census of Ireland, 1851, part V

The 1846 potato crop turned black and rotten after it had been harvested and stored. Potato blight devastates a crop after it has come to fruition. But the 1846 blight did not immediately create panic or complete despair. It meant a long and hungry winter, but that was no new thing to Ireland's peasantry. Many serious blights had occurred before, including the years 1836–7 and 1839.† It was the repetition of the blight, its recurrence year

*Hardly surprisingly, there is a considerable literature dealing with the relative importance of the famine itself in causing the change which took place around the time of the famine. As well as K. H. Connell, op. cit., and Michael Drake, op. cit., see R. Dudley Edwards and T. Desmond Williams (eds.), The Great Famine, Dublin, 1956.

†Blights had also occurred in 1728, 1739, 1770 and 1800. See Cecil Woodham Smith, The Great Hunger, London, 1962.

after year in every part of the country until 1851, which created
protracted and disastrous famine.

Five years without an autumn potato harvest entailed five
winters and springs of near or complete starvation. Only the
provision of relief by local landlords or Westminster's emergency
measures stood between millions of country people and a slow
death from hunger. Until help came the worst hunger could
temporarily be assuaged by whatever livestock, poultry and farm
animals could be eaten or sold. After that – and without milk or
eggs – came the domestic pets, berries, nettles, roots, weeds.
Without potatoes the tiny holdings of large families, the product
of sub-division and early marriage, could offer virtually nothing.
The few areas with both the skills and the resource could live
for a time on fish. But even there the situation became more and
more desperate as each year the blight reappeared.

After much resistance, born of dogmatism, cynicism, in-
credulity and indifference, the English government finally put
relief measures into effect.* Public works – the construction of
roads, railways and canals – were ordered. Behind this order
lay an economic theory: employment would lead to money, and
money would lead to markets. The forces of supply and demand
would guarantee that traders would station themselves in those
markets. It followed from this theory that starvation could not
occur if the starving had incomes. Perhaps at no time in the
history of this theory have its misconceptions been so exposed
and the tenacity of its proponents more bitterly paid for than
during the great famine.†

* In a letter of 1849 J. S. Mill expressed an almost prophetic view of
Westminster's response to Ireland's famine conditions: 'You ask what
I think of the Irish measures. I expect nothing from them but mischief,
or if any good, only through excess of evil' (quoted by J. E. Pomfret,
The Struggle for Land in Ireland, Princeton, 1930).

† J. E. Pomfret quotes E. H. Dame's *The Victorian Illusion*: 'Victorian economics were initiated, like so much else Victorian, by stolid
adherence to rule of thumb. The Victorians were always suffering for

At Vicarstown, Queen's County ... 30 gallons, or 120 quarts, of
soup were made for well under 1d. a quart ... the ingredients were
one ox head without the tongue, 28 lb. turnips, 3½ lb. onions, 7 lb.
carrots, 21 lb. pea meal, 14 lb. Indian corn-meal, and the rest water.
The local school master described the mixture as a 'vile compound',
and the people after one trial refused to accept it, declaring it gave
them bowel complaints'.

Cecil Woodham Smith: The Great Hunger

Money from employment was little enough, and certainly
could hardly pay for sufficient government-supplied grain.
Theory dictated that a low price could only wreck the market
into which so many imaginary entrepreneurs were thought to be
rushing. Hardly any entrepreneurs calculated that gains from
famine conditions would outweigh the disutilities of distance
and the short run (famine, after all, cannot go on making profits
for very long). Further, work on public projects took time, and
resulted in shortages of labour on the farms, which in turn meant
that alternative crops to potatoes were not cultivated. By the
same token turf was not cut and hauled from the bog. Indeed
many of the men had to travel great distances to get to work each
day. Soup kitchens were set up in a few locations, but the
nutritional value of the soup was small, 'not so much soup for
the poor as poor soup'.

The brutal power of nineteenth-century liberal ideas about
the sacrosanct role of free enterprise and the market force added
to the English conviction that Ireland was troublesome and
dangerous, deserving of no pity – still less of any energetic
provison of relief. Between them, these factors allowed the
famine to follow its course for three seasons. After that, the
cries of destitute Ireland plus the voice of more directly humani-

their faith that a principle, once discovered, must needs be of universal
application' (op. cit., p. 48).

tarian opinion in England were heard. By that time, however, the situation could scarcely be remedied with the speed and determination required. And even then the translation of sympathy into action was not simple and certainly not speedy. Moreover, to the dreadful consequences of the blight itself was added a succession of extraordinarily long and hard winters. For many months each year of the blight, families with neither food nor fuel crowded into their homes and shelters, freezing as well as starving. Between 1846 and 1851 approximately one million people emigrated, and at least one and a half million died of hunger or diseases precipitated by famine conditions.

After the famine it quickly became apparent that rural Ireland was irreversibly changed. The scourge of English colonization and landlordism had finally struck directly at the peasantry as, in preceding centuries, it had struck at the Gaelic lords. The famine marked the end of the truly traditional life, and signified a new struggle against English landlordism. This struggle in turn created a final onslaught by the English against Gaelic elements in the Irish colony. The peasantry by the end of the famine had revised and reversed much of their pre-famine social system, and had evolved a new and distinctive socio-economic formula for endurance. In essence, the new system arose out of a determined refusal to abandon the land. A tenacious attitude to land created on the one hand a new consciousness of landlord-peasant relationships, and on the other hand brought an end to sub-division. Fathers ceased to be willing to give land to sons who wanted to set up on their own.

The unparalleled destitution and suffering of the Irish peasantry are an instructive example of the lengths to which the landlords and the liberal bourgeoisie of a 'dominant' nation will go.

V. I. Lenin: *The British Liberals and Ireland*

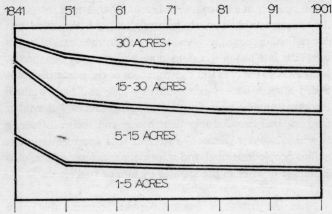

Figure 5. Distribution of agricultural land between holdings of
various sizes, 1841–1901
Source: Irish Census, 1911

Figures 5 and 6 give some idea of how agricultural holdings
and farm practice changed in the decades immediately following
the famine. But consolidation of holdings also meant a new
situation in the peasant family. During the earlier period of
rampant sub-division, when a son could maintain a family
with little more than a potato field, and such patches of land
were freely given, it was possible for him to offer his prospective
bride a farm home as soon as the young people wished to marry.
Just as the earlier practice encouraged very early marriage, so
the later practice of consolidation prevented it. Young men were
still unable to marry before they had secured a farm, and now
they were unable to secure a farm with the same ease. Refusal
to divide up the family farm also meant that only one son could
inherit. K. H. Connell notes that 'in the two or three generations
following 1780 peasant children, by and large, married whom they
pleased when they pleased'.* By the mid nineteenth century the

* See K. H. Connell, 'Peasant Marriage in Ireland after the Great
Famine', *Past and Present*, 12, 1957, pp. 76–92.

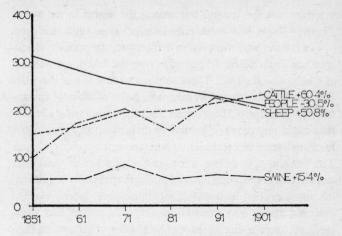

Figure 6. Densities of people and livestock per 1,000 acres of arable land, 1851–1901

Source: W. P. Coyne, ed.: *Ireland Industrial and Agricultural*

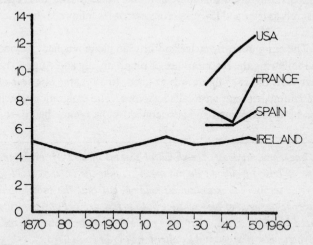

Figure 7. Crude marriage rates per 1,000 of population, 1870–1956

Source: Irish Censuses, 1911–56

marriage rate for Ireland was among the lowest in the world. Figure 7 shows how those rates have persisted since that time.

For the son who was to inherit, therefore, the price of inheritance was a much-delayed marriage, with the delaying time spent as a helper on the land. Those sons not willing to pay this price or unlikely to be chosen as inheritor, had a number of alternatives open to them. They could elect for a life in the Church; they could buy or rent a holding of their own; they could move to an Irish town and seek employment there; they could emigrate. The first was open only to a few, and required a self-confidence and interest in schooling unusual among the peasantry's children; buying or renting land was almost impossible: money was not available and it was precisely during this period that many landlords were trying to reduce the number of tenants on their estates; some did move to Irish cities, but opportunities there were few, while those ready to leave the land were attracted by emigration to America, where relatives and friends had already settled. Emigration followed the trend towards later marriages as surely as later and less numerous marriages followed reluctance to sub-divide.

The emigration from Ireland in 1846 alone reached 106,000 and following the reappearance of blight in July and August the next year, the 1847 figure was 215,000. In 1851, the last year of the famine, emigration totalled 250,000. The emigration which was both precipitated and accelerated by the famine had in the

---

In one sense, at least, the dreadful seasons of 1845–9 broke the back of Irish farming. I do not mean ... that the tenant ceased to struggle seriously to maintain his holding, but that the catastrophe ... broke the back of his exclusive passion for survival at home, and forced him to recognize that there was a deus ex machina *at hand, a practicable, if unpalatable, alternative to be considered.*

Oliver MacDonagh: *Ireland*

---

poorest regions the quality of flight – flight which was no doubt enhanced by awareness of possibilities in other milieux, but which nonetheless had its roots in devastation at home.

Yet the famine does not mark the point in Irish history where emigration assumed its modern character. The character of emigration today, and in its recent past, is quite different. The famine did not weaken the Irish country people's desire to live in Ireland. What it did do was to force a number of adaptive changes upon peasant society. That is to say, the end of sub-division and the reversal of the trend towards early marriage both signify an alteration in social practice which *facilitated* survival on the land. The famine certainly caused a loss of confidence in many features of traditional social practice. Once practice was revised, however, peasant life could continue. Although many hundreds of thousands of people were forced off the land and out of the country, the traditional determination of the Irish peasant to remain on his land persisted. In recent years emigration has derived from a revision in attitude towards rural life itself. The countryman of today usually does not want to live on the land at all, but does so as a matter of duty. For at least eighty years after the famine, life on the land was preferred to life away from the land, and it was towards staying on the land that all change was directed.*

But consolidated holdings did not in themselves provide real security against potato blight. So long as the Irish countryman

* The large size of families in many European peasant societies entailed population movement. But emigration itself was widely regarded as helpful to a society or even to the home status of the migrant. It has been noted of the European peasantry as a whole: 'Seasonal migration was not an escape from the peasant family, but a condition of its survival. The peasant went, not to acquire a new occupation in a different society, but to improve his position in the old.' H. J. Habakkuk, 'Family Structure and Economic Change in Nine-teenth-Century Europe', in N. W. Bell and E. F. Vogel (eds.), *The Family*, London, 1961.

based his subsistence on the potato, whatever the size or topography of his farm, he remained acutely vulnerable to crop failure. There is some evidence that the farmers did attempt a change in their pattern of farming. Even in Counties Mayo and Kerry – the two worst hit by famine – land under cultivation increased between 1841 and 1851 by 37 and 22 per cent respectively. Over Ireland as a whole the number of cattle and horses increased substantially between 1851 and 1901. These increases in livestock and cultivated land at a time of declining population show how the adjustment in social practice was accompanied by some adjustment in farming.*

This adjustment meant an expanded role for markets or fairs throughout the country. But the truth is that real improvements in economic conditions came to farmers on the best land. The small peasant farmers of the west coast remained largely dependent on the potato. The consolidation of holdings, even in the remotest areas, checked any increases in vulnerability and allowed farmers with money for investment in cattle to provide against any complete disaster. But when the blight struck in 1879, there was famine once again in the west. Despite the fact that between 1846 and 1864 emigrants sent some £13,000,000 to their families in Ireland, the country people of the western seaboard remained in conditions of extreme poverty. Yet with the determination and resilience characteristic of the aftermath of earlier devastations, the peasantry made their adjustment and continued to lament the emigration these adjustments entailed.

The reason for the limited extent of post-famine agricultural reconstruction lies in the limited money available for investment in the countryside. The Act of Union in 1801 brought free

* See Figures 3 and 4, pp. 35 and 52. These changes are documented very fully in W. M. Micks, *The History of the Congested Districts Board* (Dublin, 1925) and in William P. Coyne (ed.), *Ireland Industrial and Agricultural* (Dublin: Dept of Agriculture, 1909).

Do not make an union with us, Sir. We should unite with you,
only to rob you.

Dr Johnson, 1779

One by one each of our nascent industries was either strangled in its
birth or handed over gagged and bound to the jealous custody of
rival interest in England, until at last every fountain of wealth was
hermetically sealed.

Lord Dufferin: *Irish Emigration and the*
Tenure of Land in Ireland

trade between England and Ireland, and had been heralded with
altruistic noises, including the confident assertion that union
would bring English investments in Ireland. What in fact it
brought was the deterioration of Ireland's industry and virtually
no investment from England. High unemployment in the towns
meant that less money spread into the countryside, and the use
of Ireland as a convenient market for English surplus was
continuously detrimental to Irish economic development. Also,
the small amounts of money which the farmers did earn by
selling cattle were largely spent on rents instead of improvements.* And the recurrent agricultural depressions in England
in the nineteenth century periodically dried up even that source
of income.

To this situation must be added the role of the Roman
Catholic Church. It has been argued that economic development

---

*Rents were of course paid to landlords who for the most part
lived in England. Money taken from the poor farmers thus went to
help economic development in England. Further, as landlords became
uneasy about the unrest among their tenants they systematically tried
to give their better land to cattle and sheep, using higher rents and
then large-scale eviction to force the peasantry off their estates and
onto the poorer land, and thereby reducing the possibility of substantial
agricultural development which could have been of advantage to Irish
farmers.

in Ireland in the nineteenth century was primarily inhibited by the extent to which the Church remorselessy drained off all remaining surplus from each and every family.* In that way money for development was directed from farm and industry to clergy and Church. The scale of Church spending was vast indeed. Between 1800 and 1863 no fewer than 1,805 churches, 217 convents and 40 colleges and seminaries were built in Ireland. The total cost of this building was £4,428,800. And as well as financing all that building, the Church was coming to support an ever larger number of priests, monks and nuns. Their ratio to the Catholic population increased between 1850 and 1900 from 1 in 1,000 to 1 in 255.† Much of this vastly increased Church expenditure in the nineteenth century was financed by the poorest farmers of the west.

In 1881 an Act of Parliament in Westminster established the Congested Districts Board. The Board was created in response to the increasing awareness that many parts of rural Ireland – especially along the western seaboard – were still chronically overpopulated and seriously short of economic resources. It continued functioning until the end of Union in 1921. It is no coincidence that the Board was constituted at a time when Ireland's political opposition to the Act of Union was finding some echoes in England.

The Board began by determining which districts had the

* The Church of Ireland was also supported in the nineteenth century by compulsory tithes imposed on the population of every parish. It is probable that this imposition augmented the Roman Catholic Church's ability to collect voluntary monies by bringing a symbolic and political quality to support for the indigenous religion and its officers.

† For these and other fascinating details see Emmet Larkin, 'Economic Growth, Capital Investment and the Roman Catholic Church in Nineteenth-Century Ireland', *American History Review* LXXII, 3, 1967, pp. 852–84.

highest concentration of unviable holdings. In its preliminary findings the Board acknowledged one process which had been continuing for at least a century – the concentration of densest population in the least fertile areas. In those regions families could survive and pay their rents only with the help of secondary sources of income. Hence the main objectives of the Board included the purchase of land for redistribution, the improving of stocks of all farm animals, the introduction of more modern techniques through grant and instruction, the establishment of a sound fishery, the provision of loan facilities to farmers who wished to embark upon enterprises of their own, and the introduction of savings banks in the rural districts.*

Among the Board's objectives, and one which was determined in principle at the inception of the work, was the purchase and amalgamation of holdings. This entailed the contraction of the number of farm families that subsisted on any given area of land – some families were to be offered the opportunity of selling up and leaving. For such families the Board intended to provide the chance of emigration. Since emigration rates remained at a high level throughout the period of the Board's activities, it was to be expected that this element of their work would have singular importance and that the offer of emigration and sale would be taken by many farm-holders. In the history of the Board, however, it is noted that in not a single case was the interest in a holding purchased, as no tenants were willing to

* Horace Plunkett said in 1915: 'The Congested Districts, where the Board's operations are advanced, are marvellously improved. The ... defect I see is the utter ignoring of the social aspects of the problem. No attempt is made to build up rural communities' (quoted by J. J. Johnston, *Irish Agriculture in Transition*, Oxford University Press, 1951). But the *social* life does seem to have been rich. What Plunkett probably had in mind were political issues – landlordism and the acute traditional individualism the system had fostered. For detailed statistics of the Board's successes see W. M. Micks, op. cit. Micks was involved with the Board from its inception.

sell. It was decided by the Board that they would not assist in the emigration of tenants.

The supposition that tenants would sell and emigrate was based on the view that emigration could be used as an index of dissatisfaction with peasant life. Again it is to be seen that at this time emigration indicated no such thing and reflected a refusal to sub-divide rather than a refusal to farm. And the decision not to sub-divide was taken by an authoritative father who insisted on the *retention* of peasant life, preferring to exclude all but one of his sons from the holding rather than put his whole way of life at risk. There were too few farms for the people rather than an abundance of people who inclined against making use of the farms.

The peasantry certainly maintained their morale at least until the Congested Districts Board was terminated in 1921. In 1923 the Irish Free State passed and put into effect the Land Act which finally converted even the poorest tenant into an owner-occupier. That Act and the establishment of the Free State itself can only have enhanced the vitality of the country people: since the famine bitterness in the countryside against Union had been growing, and the peasantry played an active role in guerrilla actions against British troops in the rural districts, especially in the southwest.

During 1925 the new Irish government collected evidence for a report on the Gaelic-speaking parts of the country. The *Gaeltacht Report* marks the beginning of active involvement on the part of all successive Irish governments with the use of the Irish language.* But the *Report* dwells at considerable length on the economic conditions of the western districts which had always been the stronghold of the Irish speakers. Of the economic conditions, the *Report* notes: 'It appears to have been a defect in the work of the Congested Districts Board ... that the really serious areas of congestion were left without any effective

* *Gaeltacht Report*, Dublin, 1926.

Over here in England I'm helping wi' the hay
An' I wish I was in Ireland the livelong day.
Weary on the English an' sorra take the wheat!
Och! Corrymeela, an' the blue sky over it.
The people that's in England is richer nor the Jews,
There's not the smallest young gossoon but threads in his shoes!
I'd give the pipe between my teeth to see a barefoot child,
Och! Corrymeela, an' the low south wind.
D'ye mind me now, the song at night is mortal hard to raise,
The girls are heavy goin' here, the boys are ill to plase,
When ones't I'm out this workin' hive, 'tis I'll be back again –
Aye, Corrymeela in the same soft rain.

'Corrymeela – a Peasant Lament' quoted by W. B. Yeats:
The Irish Literary Revival

measures being taken to improve them, and effort was concentrated on less needy districts where quicker returns were obtainable.' Generally the *Report* insists, as had the Board in 1894, that the peasantry of the west, most particularly the Gaelic-speaking districts, were still able to survive on their land only through seasonal migration and other secondary sources of income. Patrick Gallagher's evidence to the Commission, while explicitly concerned with the Rosses region of Donegal, is the theme of the *Report* as a whole: Gallagher affirmed that 'people look upon the little holding at home as a place to come to for a few months in the winter, some place in which to build a nest, while they look to Scotland, the Lagan and America as the place in which to earn the money to keep the rest'. Poverty persisted and farm families had to look beyond their farms for an income without which they could not endure. But nowhere in the *Gaeltacht Report* is it suggested that the country people are demoralized.

That the Irish country people were not demoralized, and

had in fact established a new style of country life which included the older folk tradition of singing, dancing, storytelling and mutual aid, is shown by the literature from 1900 to 1940. Throughout the writings of Synge, O'Sullivan, Pat Mullen and many others there are vivid descriptions of a highly sociable and vivacious country life. Only in the last years – the tensions of a young couple who had to decide their commitment to their western home, or in the final depopulation of the Blaskets – does any sense of the impending demoralization obtrude.* What is now termed traditional life was evidently a source of gaiety and co-operation at least until the time of the Second World War.

But the next substantial account gives a very different picture. Between 1948 and 1954, when the Irish government was becoming alarmed by the persistently high rate at which the most traditional parts of Ireland were becoming depopulated, a Commission collected information on the background and circumstances of emigration throughout the country. Their findings were published in Dublin in 1956 as *The Commission on Emigration and Other Population Problems*. A key to them lies in this passage: 'We were impressed by the unanimity of the views presented to us in the evidence on the relative loneliness, dullness and general unattractive nature of life in many parts of rural Ireland at present' (p. 175). Further, the Commission on Emigration disavows the strict connection between emigration and the economy at home. 'To state that emigration is due to lack of economic development at home is true only in the sense of a truism' (p. 202).

The Commission is particularly concerned with the country people's sense of relative deprivation and disadvantage – relative to the cities to which they and their relatives have

*Peadar O'Donnell's novel *Islanders* (London, 1928) was probably the first book about life in the west of Ireland which focused on the difficult choice for young people between life at home in the west and a more 'sophisticated' urban life.

migrated. But the evidence upon which the opinions of the Commission are based was collected at a particularly significant juncture in the history of rural emigration. Labour opportunities in England and America suddenly expanded in the late 1930s with the end of the depression. Rural electrification had reached all but the remote districts by 1948, bringing radio, cinema and eventually television, all of which must have reacted strongly upon the imagination of the potential emigrant and the social system he was leaving. The market for both salted and fresh mackerel upon which much of the western fishery depended, particularly in the smaller centres, collapsed in the 1930s. A new economic contraction, therefore, combined with vastly improved communications and a corresponding limitation of traditional social life to create a situation in which emigration was likely to increase suddenly in the more traditional and isolated regions. By the time the Commission wrote up its evidence a new emigration had rebounded upon the rural communities, and involved them in that sense of isolation and disadvantage which corresponds to a new commitment to urban standards and a more urban way of life. This emigration was new. For the first time in Irish history it did reflect a definite preference for another way of life. The peasants' determination to stay on the land seemed to have broken.

Both decline and imbalance in population continue to dominate rural Ireland. There has been a persistence, therefore, in both demographic and social factors since the famine. But the persistence itself must not be seen as indication of a fundamentally unchanged situation. The communities adjusted in the aftermath of the famine and considerably revised their social and economic practice, thereby securing and perpetuating the peasant life. This determination to remain on the land lasted through the nineteenth century, and is reflected in the form assumed by the people's response to the Congested Districts Board. From 1850 to 1925 the peasantry of rural Ireland did not conceive of peasant

life as oppressively disadvantaged, nor did they associate life in
the countryside with some kind of failure or loss of opportunity.

That sense of relative deprivation emerged at the earliest in
the period just prior to the Second World War. It was then that
the qualities of emigration and rural life alike were irrevocably
altered. Today almost a majority of country people of the remoter
districts find their way of life a burden to be avoided if possible.
The farmer of today tends to locate his life by comparison with
another way of life – one, moreover, that he regards as intrinsic-
ally more rewarding. As this new situation has developed, so
community life has been profoundly altered.

Throughout the difficult period following the famine, alongside the limited endeavours of the Congested Districts Board,
into the first decades of the Irish Free State's existence, the
peasantry of the infertile west sought above all to hold on to
their farms. Generation after generation of emigrants were
forced out of the countryside because farmers would not break
up their holdings. Change which entailed the abandonment of
holdings was doomed to a peripheral role in the history of the
countryside. In the past thirty years that has been reversed: at

---

'Well, father,' said I, and he on the other side of the fire reading a
letter which had come that day from America, 'what is your opinion
of the great long journey that is now before me?'

'When will you be going?' said he with a sigh.

'Tomorrow.'

'Well, I give you my blessing, for so far as this place is concerned
there is no doubt but it is gone to ruin.'

'It is, long since, and even if it were not, what is in it but fishing,
hunting and fowling, and according to the old saying they are the
three most unprofitable occupations!'

'It is true,' he said sadly, and he returned to his reading.

　　　　　　　　　Maurice O'Sullivan: Twenty Years A-Growing

---

present it is changes requiring the householders' tenacity and optimism which can make no headway. It is a demoralized population which endures the hardship of rural life in the west of Ireland today.

In the past two censuses the population of Ireland as a whole has at last ceased to decline. But those statistics are national and as Figure 8 shows the steady drain of people away from the western seaboard is continuing. The rate is scarcely abated. The next chapter describes one parish. Inishkillane exemplifies in all its details the majority of villages and communities which, in vestigial form, spread still from Bantry Bay to Tory Island.

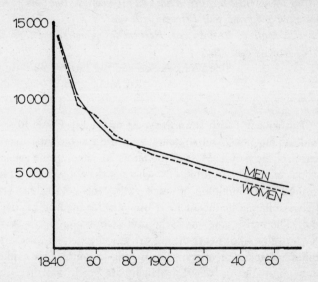

Figure 8. Total population of men and women of eleven electoral divisions in the west of Ireland, 1841–1966
Source: Irish Censuses, 1841–1966

3 Inishkillane

'No, Avic,' she replied. 'An old stalk thrives but ill when trans-
planted. No matter what happens ... I'll be happier here in Erin,
sitting by my little turf fire in my own little corner. But come to see
me often and bring your Princess with you.'
'I will, Mother,' he answered. He kept his promise, and they all
lived happily ever after.
                              'The Widow's Son and the Little Tailor' from
                              Pat Mullen (ed.): Irish Tales

Inishkillane parish is on the coast of County Clare. Rough
and mountainous land stretches from the shore to the inland
edges of the parish. Most of the farms are sited on the rugged
slopes of steep coastal hills. Nowhere is there a valley of level
ground. The multitude of stone walls, lanes, old cabins and
houses, all indicate the intensive use to which the land has been
put. The parish is isolated: the nearest bus-stop is in a small
town twelve miles away; the railway was never closer than forty
miles and today the nearest functioning station is eighty miles
away. But the roads to Inishkillane are good, and there are
mountain paths to the nearest market town. Farmers taking their
cattle to market can set out over the mountain when the bars
close and arrive by six in the morning. In all these ways Inishkillane is much like many hundreds of parishes along Ireland's
west coast.

The population declines which Inishkillane has experienced

are also typical. In 1843 there were 209 baptisms in the parish.
In 1893 there were 63; by 1923 the number had fallen to 44. In
1963 only 19 children were born in Inishkillane.* The economic
disturbances and reverses accompanying this decline began with
the famine, but the community was still populous and resilient
at the end of the century: between 1891 and 1911 the number of
parishioners did fall from 6,800 to 5,500, but over the same period
the Congested Districts Board built three jetties and success-
fully encouraged the Inishkillane men to turn to fishing as an
economic mainstay.

The curing of mackerel for export began in the west of
Ireland in 1887. The trade was good for coastal parishes. The
fish lay close to the shore, and were best taken in seine nets from
small light boats. Not much capital was needed for this business.
Salting and barrelling was done at the pier-heads of new jetties
by local women. Middle-men in the villages negotiated orders
and delivery dates with foreign buyers. In the 1905–6 season
30,800 barrels of cured mackerel were sold from the west coast
of Ireland, from the small and poor communities all along the
Atlantic coast, to American, Norwegian and English buyers.
The trade continued thriving for twenty years, the fishermen

---

*The autumn fishery which begins in the end of August often lasts
on ... into the winter, and up to Christmas. It is a row-boat and
canoe fishery.... It is also widespread in its distribution, almost
every creek from the south of Cork to the north of Mayo taking part
in it.*

William P. Coyne (ed.): *Ireland Agricultural and Industrial*

---

*All statistical data in this chapter on baptisms and marriages came
from Inishkillane parish records and census returns. The more detailed
data on households were compiled from notebooks and records kept by
three successive Inishkillane parish priests. Some additional data came
from registers and reports kept by the Inishkillane school teachers.

earning between £50 and £100 per season.* (In 1920 porter cost
2d. a pint and whiskey 1s. 6d. a half pint.)

The history of the Inishkillane fishing gives a picture of an
important fifteen years in the parish's recent past. It illustrates
the enthusiasm with which local people embraced new economic
opportunities in the earlier part of this century, and shows in
some detail that people were not demoralized at that time, that
they had not jettisoned their determination to stay at home on the
land. And the fishery was above all a way of staying on the land,
for it bolstered a subsistence economy by enabling householders
to pay rent on their holdings and buy the minimum of necessary
supplementary goods. The proportion of Inishkillane householders who turned to fishing to subsidize their farming, and
the determination and efficiency with which they fished, showed
how determined they were to stay on the land. There is one
sure sign that fishing never displaced land as the social and
economic mainstay at the heart of Inishkillane life: even at the
height of the fishery, when demand for the fish seemed boundless with prices high and reliable, those young men who were
not heirs to land could not find wives in the parish. Fishing did
not stop the kind of emigration which had developed in the
aftermath of the great famine. The Inishkillane fishery is something of an index of the resilience and continuity of Inishkillane
peasant society, though its eventual decline also shows how
vulnerable Inishkillane people were made to vicissitudes in
social and economic life far beyond their own boundaries.

In 1925 Inishkillane harboured seventeen crews of fishermen, all involved in close shore seine-netting for the mackerel
trade. They supported their earnings from salted mackerel with
herring and lobsters. But the monetary value of the mackerel

---

*For information on the fishery at this period see *Report of the
Chief Inspector of Fisheries*, Dept of Agriculture and Technical Instruc-
tion, Dublin, 1907; *West Cork Resource Survey*, Dublin, 1963; and the
Gaeltacht Report, Dublin, 1926.

catch was six times greater than the herring, while white fish –
today the most valuable fishing resource in these regions – was
virtually worthless. A seine crew usually totalled fifteen men,
twelve in one boat and three in a second. The nets were set at
dusk and the fish landed in the morning for curing. This fishing
employed at least 250 men and 100 women for part of the
year.

But very few householders were exclusively fishermen. In 1925
for every one man in the west of Ireland who was occupied
solely with fishing, 240 were also engaged on farming or some
other employment. Fishing, however, was a central part of
parish life and for a time the single most important source of
cash earnings for many families. The large number of boats,
the regular passage along the coast to market towns, and the
identity of interest between the many crews in neighbouring
parishes, all gave movement and life to Inishkillane.

But 1925 was a bad year for the fishermen. The weather was
unusually treacherous, and the fish less abundant. Most
important, uncertainty in the market appeared for the first time.

---

to crews who carried slate: 3 bottles whisky.

> Item in account of building of
> new school in Inishkillane, 1928

34. *Are these fishermen sons of farmers? – Farmers and farmers'
sons. Every one of them has a bit of land. I know nobody who
depends on fishing alone.*

35. *Is the land the better for this dependence on the fishing? –
They don't work the land properly at all.*

36. *Would it be possible to get more out of the land? – It would.*

> Inishkillane teacher's evidence to the
> Gaeltacht Commission, October 1925

The following year many American buyers issued warnings to middle-men in the parishes of the west. In September 1926 one Inishkillane agent received a letter from the Geyer Company, exporters and importers of Baltimore, County Cork, which must have sounded ominous to the fishermen. It included this warning:

Let nobody in Ireland overlook the large catch of American mackerel and the intense activity of the Gloucester [Massachusetts] firms in trying to place these mackerel which very likely are averaging around 180 to 185 fish per barrel ... in other words it is around $6\frac{3}{4}$c per pound ... only this morning we learned from Cincinnati how our biggest friend there has just brought five cured loads of shore mackerel ...

Suddenly the trade was threatened by competition from American fishermen. But the Irish fishery was well established and could for the time being maintain a competitive position.

One particularly unpleasant consequence of the nervousness which the more highly competitive situation produced was the power of local buyers. Agents of big American and Norwegian companies would refuse to accept the prices asked for catches. The tactic was well known: the asking price was ridiculed by buyers as much too high. Then came a waiting game. Buyers just refused to negotiate, and let time itself force down the price. The fishermen could not wait too long, and gradually were compelled to accept the lowest prices. As early as 1907 there is an account of this practice by the priest of the parish adjacent to Inishkillane. He noted that the buyers 'sometimes leave the fish there from 8 o'clock in the morning for three or four hours, and the fishermen can do nothing. The fish was in their hands, and the price came down during the day to eight, six, or four shillings, and even to half a crown, but what could the fishermen do ?'*

* Quoted by the Chief Inspector of Fisheries in his *Report*, op. cit., p. 28.

Despite these warnings and the hard policies of buyers, Inishkillane fishermen managed to keep their prices low enough to stay in the American markets. Then in January 1928 a local paper carried an article discussing the rise of the Norwegian fishery, and the determination of Norwegian fishermen to place their cured mackerel and herring in markets which had for a decade or more been dominated by the Irish trade. For a time these anxious analysts and prophets were driven into the background by the high demand for Irish fish from 1929 to 1931. But the Inishkillane people were faced with the threat from the American fishery when a letter came to the largest Inishkillane agent from Booth Fisheries Company, Gloucester, Massachusetts. It was written on 2 August 1932:

Dear Mr Ryan,
    I know that you are anxious to have some definite news as regards the American mackerel situation. During the past few weeks, the fleet has found an abundance of small mackerel almost anywhere that they cared to look. Hardly a day passes when there is not a large number of vessels in port with all kinds of fares.
    There is a constant situation where the supply is in excess of the fresh fish market, and consequently, a proportionate part goes to the splitters. During the month of July the two largest firms in Gloucester have continually split these mackerel. We ourselves did not take any until yesterday...
    These mackerel ... are being purchased from the fishermen at $\frac{3}{4}$c per pound, and therefore you can see that there are going to be some very cheap mackerel on this side of which it would be impossible to compete with on a question of price.
    At the present writing, it looks very much as if these small mackerel are going to stay with us...

The price for small fish had thus dropped in six years from a little over 6c to a little under 1c a pound. The only room for the Irish fishermen in this situation was the supply of large fish, or whatever size fish the American fishermen were not succeeding in catching. The letter to Inishkillane from Massachusetts was followed nine days later by a letter from New York City. Charles F. Mattlage and Sons, importers and distributors, then wrote to the same agent:

Dear Sir,

We thank you for your letter of July 25th, and regret to say that we cannot give you very much encouragement...

The most alarming part about our whole business is the continuous decrease in interest in Salt Mackerel by the common public. This desire for salt fish has been replaced by either fresh or frozen fish, or even by canned fish, with the result that we are not selling nearly as much salted fish as in previous years. This is not a recent innovation, but it has been a slow and gradual process that has suddenly come to light and given us the realization that the sale of salt mackerel is practically over.

...Now, to outline the conditions that exist this year. Along our own shore the mackerel are very plentiful. There are a great many of them in varying sizes.... In previous years when we had a large pack of shore mackerel they all seemed to be one size and this gave the foreign producer an opportunity to produce and ship into this market sizes that the American producer did not pack, and the result was that he had a pretty good business...

The cost of the American fish because they are so plentiful are coming in to the producer at $\frac{3}{4}$c to 1c a pound. Inasmuch as it takes 300 lbs. of mackerel to make a barrel of salt mackerel, let us for argument's sake figure on the 1c a pound and give you the following figures.

Fish	$3.00
labour and splitting and salting	$2.00
cost of empty barrels and salt	$2.00
overhead and repacking	$1.00

This means the cost to the producer in this country is $8.00 a barrel. He will sell these for $10.00 a barrel. That means that the imported mackerel must sell at less than 30 shillings a barrel f.o.b. Liverpool in order to compete.

Certainly not a happy prospect. We are giving you this information to the best of our ability, and sincerely hope that it will help
you make up your mind what to do.

What the Inishkillane people did was keep on fishing,
splitting, salting and barrelling the fish. Then they tried to sell
whatever they could for whatever money they could. Because
such a large proportion of the fishermen were also farmers, and
lived a basically subsistence life, they were willing to watch the
prices fall and just take whatever money they could get. It was
never a question of the cost of fishing against some alternative
source of income. There were few real alternatives which did not
entail emigration. As fishing was threatened, so subsistence
farming became more important. The disastrously low prices
and insecure trade did not bring an end to the seine boats. In
1933 there were as many crews in Inishkillane as in 1920.

And the fishermen's tenacity and optimism were partially
justified. In 1933, after the annihilation of the salt mackerel
industry had seemed imminent, a demand did come for Inishkillane mackerel. On 14 August of that year a firm of fish smokers
in Baltimore asked their Inishkillane agent to cable their 'best
offerings', and the fishermen shipped a thousand barrels to
America in October despite some difficulties with the steamship
agents. Unfortunately I have discovered no record of the price
at which this sizeable order was sold, but the fishermen kept at

---

*It was the sight of the fishing schooners on the Grand Banks of
Newfoundland that finally roused me and turned my thoughts
definitely to America. Shouts from the passengers of, 'There they
are!' as they pointed to those crack fishing boats, and, 'We are
crossing the Banks at last!' made me realize that we were nearing
the promised land where bright golden dreams of my youth had
always been turning.*

Pat Mullen: *Come Another Day*

---

work every season for the next three years. No doubt they were getting rid of their catch at the lowest prices, and no doubt had to endure the agents' and buyers' ways of exploiting their advantage.

Those years of low prices, however, marked the end of the cured fish trade. By 1938 the Inishkillane crews had hauled their long boats for the last time. Lobster fishermen continued their summer fishing, but the majority of the men who had found cash earnings in autumn and winter fishing were forced to live entirely off their farms, or to go for some part of each year to England, or to emigrate altogether.

Of course emigration from Inishkillane had been high when the best prices were being paid for cured mackerel.* The decline in population is shown in Figure 9, and there is little sign in these emigration figures of a successful resource holding the people in the countryside during the first three decades of the century. It is important to remember that fishermen were for the most part householders. The household farm and a tradition of subsistence living were a much older and more certainly established part of Inishkillane life than fishing. The social structure of Inishkillane, as part of the tradition of peasant life in Ireland as a whole, evolved around land and farming. Even on the coast many thousands of country people died or fled because of potato blight during the eighteenth and nineteenth centuries. The Inishkillane fisherman's younger brothers could not inherit the farm, and even if they were good at fishing there was little chance of marriage without an inheritance of land. Equally, when the fishing collapsed the basis for emigration among householders was not especially increased. Some were deterred from leaving the countryside by the persistent depression in England and then by the crash in America. But surpris-

---

*In his evidence to the *Gaeltacht Report* in 1925 an Inishkillane teacher stated that many of the people had 'their eyes all the time on America' (§41).

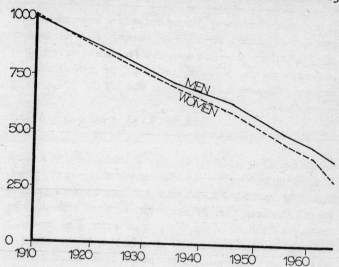

Figure 9. Total population of men and women in the electoral division including Inishkillane parish, 1910–66
Source: Parish records

ingly large numbers of young Irish men and women continued to emigrate despite the evident dearth of employment in both America and England.

This emigration was surrounded with lamentation. Its mood was still pervaded by a sense of inevitability; it was not seen as a chance for a better and brighter life. The America Wake is still remembered in Inishkillane. When a young member of the parish left for America, family and neighbours gathered in his parents' home and spent the night drinking, smoking, keening* and playing games – the four most important parts of the secular

* Keening is the Irish term for prolonged and intoned wailing. As in many other societies keening was the special duty of older women and they would maintain a more or less continuous wailing throughout the first night after a death and then during the funeral procession.

It is a strange mixture of dancing and sudden lamentation which
continues all through the night till morning. It is not without
significance that so funereal a name should be given to the emigration
ceremonies, for the Irish emigrant is not the personification of
national adventure, but of something that has the appearance of
national doom.

Robert Lynd: *Social Life in Ireland*

rituals attending death. At the edge of Inishkillane, at a sharp
bend in the lane leading out of the largest village in the parish
and on to the mountain pass, there is a huge angular rock. It is
around this rock that the lane makes its turn. It used to be
known as the Rock of the Weeping of Tears. The departing
emigrant was accompanied by 'mourners' from the village to
that rock, and their last sight of him was as he walked the lane
to that turn. It was then the long journey away from Inishkillane
began – twelve miles to the market town, a bus beyond there to
the railway, on to Cork or Dublin, and a ship for America....
Few people returned to Inishkillane after leaving, though virtually all sent money when they were able. And of course they
wrote, encouraging their younger brothers and sisters to come
and join them.

The most successful of the Inishkillane agents for American
fish buyers became an agent for shipping lines which looked for
the emigrant business. In the shop where he carried out his
buying and negotiating were hung pictures of ships, maps of
America, and advertisements of special deals to help the young
make their way to the new world. These advertisements were
sent by the shipping lines. The agent arranged for an emigrant's
complete passage – from the Rock of Tears to a city in the
United States. As the cured mackerel trade declined, so the emigration business took a slight turn for the better. But the
agents' advantage was very short-lived. Quite abruptly emigrants

began to go in large numbers to England instead of America. By the end of the Second World War, the great majority of people leaving Inishkillane headed for the cities of England, while the few who did go to America were usually sent tickets by relatives already there. Just as the negotiating of the cured fish trade vanished, so did the negotiating of emigrants' journeys.

The success of the Irish nationalist movement also brought changes to the parish. Before 1923 Inishkillane farmers paid rents to landowners. After the 1923 Land Act, they became owner occupiers paying a small fee to the Irish Free State Land Commission. In the following years the Land Commission urged more consolidation and rationalization of holdings. The rough mountain grazing was placed in commonage to named households, and the bog was divided among all the parishioners.*

'Wasn't it a great thought Columbus had,' said a man to me once as we lay gazing out over the Atlantic, 'to find out America? For if there wasn't America, the Island wouldn't stand a week.'

> quoted by Robin Flower: *The Western Island*

'Ah, poor fellow,' said she. 'I suppose he will get used to it like another; and wouldn't he be worse off if he was beyond the seas in St Louis, or the towns of America.'

> A woman speaking of a young man in England, quoted by J. M. Synge: *In Wicklow and West Kerry*

---

*Details of land-ownership, transactions and fee payments are available in the records of the rent and rate offices in Dublin. Unfortunately the Inishkillane records are extremely confused and it proved impossible to calculate the acreage of each family farm. But the sizes ranged from less than 10 to over 200 acres, with the vast majority between 30 and 70 acres. Given the large areas of steep hill and bog land size is certainly not a criterion of value or even of viability.

Every Inishkillane family thus came to have grazing and fuel. But farms were still small and infertile. At the same time political changes in Ireland as well as disruptions throughout the world brought Inishkillane into closer touch with the larger society beyond its market town. In the late 1930s the demand for labour in England revived, and Inishkillane people turned more towards England for information as well as employment.

By 1950 so many of the people of Inishkillane had turned away from the life which the parish could offer that the population began to experience serious imbalances. It is the development of these imbalances which most precisely reveals the condition of the west of Ireland today. The degree of imbalance in the Inishkillane population goes far beyond anything that previous writings on rural Ireland have indicated. I had been told by Inishkillane pessimists that the parish was seeing bad times and would see worse yet, but what I eventually discovered goes beyond anything even they had warned. It is likely that many people will be inclined to discount these stark and ominous figures; they will be said to be untypical if not actually false. But Inishkillane is representative of the majority of remote western parishes of Ireland. It is situated in typical country, has quite usual resources, and has experienced social and economic reverses as much and as little as any other place of its kind. Unfortunately, it is extremely difficult to assemble a profile of all the households in a parish, and I have not been able to compare this account of Inishkillane with similar accounts of other places. But all that I have experienced of parishes in West Cork, Connemara and West Clare leads me to think that many hundreds of other rural parishes are in much the same predicament as Inishkillane. The facts about Inishkillane match or at least adumbrate the patterns which threaten almost every isolated community in Ireland.

Today there are 231 households in the parish. An extraordinarily large number of these homes are occupied by acutely isolated people. In a sense, of course, almost every person in Inishkillane is socially isolated, and every unmarried person could be said to be sexually isolated. But if we only consider *chronic* isolation, the situation is more striking and more clear. The following circumstances can be taken as a rough criterion for social isolation: where the household comprises a person or persons who have no close kin of another generation either in the house or in the neighbourhood. The isolation is chronic where there is no possibility of the household expanding – of coming to include a new generation. Similarly, a rough criterion of sexual isolation can be that a person has no sexual or marital partner in the house or in the neighbourhood. And this is chronic where there is no realistic hope of the person ever finding such a partner.

These criteria exclude the young, married and unmarried, as well as those old people whose children have remained at home, either on the traditional farm or in the locality. One class of old people which does not readily fall into this category comprises those whose children have migrated to more distant parts of Ireland. Distance makes a great difference here, as well as the inclination in individual cases to visit the family home. But only those persons who are not visited frequently by children remaining in Ireland are included among the chronically isolated.

The Inishkillane parish population can be divided into a number of categories:

1. 32 bachelors living entirely alone
2. 4 spinsters living entirely alone
3. 3 widowers living entirely alone
4. 13 widows living entirely alone

A total of 52 people in a parish of 231 households therefore live by themselves. As well as this large number of solitary persons, there are:

    5. 21 bachelors who live with siblings
    6. 10 spinsters who live with siblings

Also there are:

    7. 11 couples who live alone
    8. 12 couples who live alone, but have married children
       locally

It emerges that in Inishkillane there are a total of 115
chronically isolated people, between them occupying 80 houses.
That is to say, approximately 35 per cent of the parish households
consist of people who have no close kin in the neighbourhood
other than an elderly brother or sister with whom they share the
family farm. None of these people can have any real hope of
enlarging their family circle.

The bachelors and spinsters living alone are all over 35. That
they are alone means that they have no relatives who can take
them in. The extended Irish family retains those unmarried
children who do not emigrate. Therefore, in all cases within the
categories 1 to 4, the individuals live in the family homes, having
been left there by death and emigration.

It is not as easy to determine a corresponding set of details
dealing with chronic sexual isolation. But a beginning can be
made by noting that most persons in the first six categories
must be included and the following facts provide a fairly complete account:

Total number of bachelors over 35: 87
Total number of spinsters over 30: 28
Total number of widowers: 3
Total number of widows: 13

Out of 436 people living in Inishkillane, therefore, a total of 131
people can be said to be chronically sexually isolated: none of
these people has a sexual partner in the house or the neighbourhood, and none can realistically expect to find one. The predica-

the young, alive, beautiful, ugly, endangered, the old, ripe, sad, and
slow; those not young, not old, drifting, confused.

Kurt H. Wolf in A. J. Vidich *et al.* (eds.)
Reflections on Community Studies

ment of this large group is made acute by the atrophy of community life: neither festive season nor traditional mutual aid
can ameliorate the loneliness. Many of the people and most of
their activities have disappeared from the countryside. The
conjunction of these changes has exposed those who remain to
ever-increasing isolation. As both social life and the very society
itself have contracted in the parish, so opportunities for ameliorat-
ing loneliness have also contracted.

The high proportion of households occupied by the chronically isolated has a corollary in a further imbalance in the
population of the parish: the preponderance of the middle-aged
and elderly. This can be illustrated by listing the twelve
categories of households inhabited by the isolated and noting
the average age of the people in each group.

1. Bachelors living entirely alone: 56
2. Spinsters living entirely alone: 61
3. Widowers living entirely alone: 68
4. Widows living entirely alone: 66
5. Bachelors living with mother: 42
6. Bachelors living with father: 42
7. Spinsters living with family: 59
8. Bachelors living with family: 47
9. Bachelors living with siblings: 62
10. Spinsters living with siblings: 64
11. Couples living alone but with
    children in the parish: 73 (m)/64 (f)
12. Couples living alone: 65 (m)/61 (f)

These twelve groups between them comprise 116 farms. The remaining 115 households in the parish include children, but only 80 of them have children of school age or younger. Perhaps even more striking, there are only 46 farms in the entire parish with children who are at home and helping with the farm work. The significance of this figure lies, of course, in its implications for the future: the next generation of farmers would normally be formed by those who stayed home to help. In the present situation it seems that only 20 per cent of the parish farms have much chance of lasting another generation.

The middle-aged and the elderly, therefore, have possession of over half the houses in the parish. In none of these houses is there any real possibility of a younger generation emerging. The imbalance in the age structure of the parish population is shown in Figure 10. The remarkable fact is that the 46–70 age group outnumbers the 15–40 by more than 2 to 1. And in the entire parish there are only 64 young people who have left school, remain unmarried, and who may yet get married.

Despite the decline and imbalance in the population of the parish, the birth rate of the families has remained high. Although there is a vast difference between nineteenth-century and contemporary figures – 6,768 children were born in Inishkillane between 1837 and 1887, compared with 1,498 between 1912 and 1962 – the number of children per marriage has fluctuated very little. But the constant rate of baptisms suggests that the number of households was remaining more or less constant; where families were large, the price paid for this constant was continuously high emigration rates. Moreover, the age structure of the community and the large proportion of households which do not include the next generation means that such an even level cannot be maintained. And when the details of present age structure are seen alongside recent rates of childbirth it becomes evident just how large a proportion of each generation has been leaving the parish.

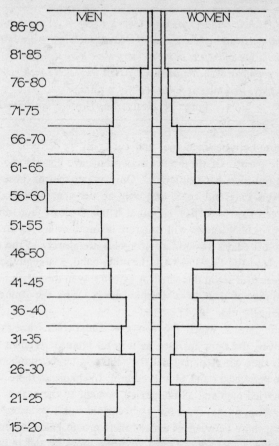

Figure 10. Proportion of men and women living in Inishkillane parish for each five-year age group, 15–90
Source: Parish records

By comparing the people of various age groups living in the parish today with the baptismal record, it is possible to calculate very approximately what percentage of each generation has remained on the land. The results indicate a continual decline:

Today whole villages around Charlestown – for centuries the spawning streams of the people of Mayo and Sligo – are silted by depopulation and where in my memory there were shoals of children, more populous than the salmon parr in the town's rich river, no child plays and there is no promise of a child.

James N. Healy: *The Death of an Irish Town*

of those born between 1908 and 1915 only 33 per cent are still in the parish. Of the 67 per cent who have gone, some have died, but most have emigrated. Only 25 per cent of those born between 1923 and 1928, and only 20 per cent of those born between 1940 and 1945, stayed at home. At least four fifths of today's school leavers will emigrate before they are 30. Indeed, many of today's 16- and 17-year-olds are already in the cities of Ireland and England.* On the other hand, a large proportion of those who are in the parish at 35 will stay in the parish for the remainder of their lives. Inishkillane is losing the young and keeping the old.

The rate at which the young of the parish leave is not, however, the same for men as it is for women. Women leave when they are younger, and they leave in larger numbers. Of those between 15 and 35 at present in Inishkillane, there are 49 unmarried men and 28 unmarried women. In the next 20-year age group, 35–55, there are 35 bachelors and 6 spinsters. And among those between 55 and 75 there are 39 bachelors and 17 spinsters. There are two possible explanations for this in purely demographic terms: either the women are choosing husbands from other parishes, or they are emigrating. In either case, they

* The Inishkillane priest did his own survey in 1969 of the proportion of emigrants in each generation. His figures were compiled from discussions with families. They vary from mine only in the most recent group; he found that nearly 90 per cent of those born between 1940 and 1945 had already emigrated.

are deciding that it is better not to be in the parish, married or unmarried. On the other hand, the men have been more inclined to be unmarried in Inishkillane than married abroad. Families tend to expect that at least one son will remain at home to keep the farm going. This pressure in itself could account for the comparative success the community has had in retaining its sons. It is easier for the last girl at home to decide to leave than it is for the last boy.

Since the girls now refuse to stay in the countryside, the last son of a family who stays at home is unlikely to marry. In the parish today, therefore, one son in each family is faced with a choice between staying celibate at home and emigrating with the chance of marriage. The parish girls are strongly opposed to marrying local people. They do not want a life on the farm, and they *do* want to discover life in the city. Traditionally, a girl was married in her own parish church, even if the husband was from another parish. It follows that the parish marriage register provides an accurate indication of the number of Inishkillane girls who decided to marry and settle down locally – girls who marry Englishmen almost always marry in England. Not a single marriage occurred in 1959, for the first time in the 150 years of the parish's recorded history. Between 1954 and 1958 only 21 marriages were celebrated – barely four for each year. But between 1959 and 1963 the total dropped to 9, and between 1963 and 1968 dropped again, to 7. There is no reason for expecting the numbers to climb. Inishkillane teenage girls openly and remorselessly scorn the possibility of marrying a local. The bond between the young women of the parish and the traditional life has snapped almost completely. Some girls dutifully return for Christmas and summer holidays, but virtually none come to marry.

Of those now married and living in Inishkillane, 80 per cent married in the parish church. Since a wedding is solemnized in the bride's parish church, it follows that 80 per cent of

Inishkillane couples married within the parish. Assuming this
to be the pattern for all the parishes in the neighbourhood, it also
follows that a girl usually either married in her home parish or
moved away altogether. Hence, the young farmer was confronted by a simple alternative – find a girl at home or find one
far away. As finding a girl at home became less and less possible,
so a large group of bachelors – far outnumbering spinsters – was
created. The preponderance of men throughout rural Ireland is
indicated in Figure 11.* Obviously, the statistical dominance
of the old and of men is a precise corollary of sexual and social
isolation. Moreover, as the situation has developed, so the
separate factors have aggravated one another: each new group
of school-leavers has been confronted by a more strikingly
imbalanced population, and that has made each successive group
less likely to stay at home on the land.

It is true that a small number of men return to their native
parish after some years in England or America. Among the older
men in Inishkillane there are some who have spent as much as
fifteen years away, and then returned to the family farm. At the
edge of one of Inishkillane's villages there stands a small old-
fashioned cottage. It was inhabited by a farming family whose
small fields lay between the cottage and the sea. Eventually the
farm was left to an unmarried son. The other children had gone
away and the parents died. For some years the son lived alone in
the family home and maintained the family lands as well as he
was able. One morning in 1952 he decided to leave. He had made
no preparations, but simply left the breakfast table, put on his
boots, gathered his savings and a few bare essentials together,

*An article in the *Irish Times* gives some very remarkable statistics
on the ratio of men to women in the aggregate of rural areas in Ireland:

Females per 1,000 Males in Age Groups, 1966

15–24	25–34	35–44
738	423	375

See 'Change in the Gaeltacht, 3: Patterns of Emigration', *Irish Times*,
2 April, 1971.

been in Inishkillane when he was a little over twenty. Returning
after those years was a tremendous shock to him. He told how
the silence of the landscape itself oppressed him and how his life
in Chicago would keep returning to his thoughts. He said that
for the first five years after returning he was unable to talk to
anyone, and recalled the old joke: 'Aye, they say the first seven
years are the worst.'

It is now fifteen years since he returned. He maintains the
farm, keeping three cows and attending a good garden of
vegetables. He cuts and draws his turf off a mountain bog. He
has been a dutiful son. But at forty-nine he is a bachelor in ever-
growing isolation. His mother will not live much longer, and
soon he will be alone on the farm, in a situation he abandoned
some thirty years earlier because it did not offer the kind of life
and opportunity he had come to desire. Thirty years later the
decline in community life has proceeded, and the loneliness of
the unmarried farmer is so much the greater.

Some men in the west have attempted to overcome the problem created by a conflict between the hopes of their old parents
and their own needs by coming home for the summer and doing
seasonal work in England. These men return to the parish in
late June and stay until September. Their stay coincides with
haymaking and lobster fishing. It also coincides with the tourist
season, and Inishkillane – like almost all western parishes – has
a number of guest houses which fill for the summer holidays.
But this annual migration can be adopted only by young men
who take unskilled work which they can easily leave and resume
at will. Further, it depends on a very high level of employment
in England: most of the migrants work on building sites in the
winter, and construction work is always easier to find in summer.
But when these conditions are met, some old people in the parish
are protected against a year of unbroken isolation by their sons'
mobility.

Yet they are few. Far more frequently a household is made up of either old people alone or bachelor children who have remained on the land to save their parents from a lonely and helpless old age and the land itself from final abandonment. The young who remained at home used to inherit a farm, but today they inherit more isolation than land. The Inishkillane community is intensely demoralized. The new generation does not benefit from the post-famine adaptations, but is composed instead of people who are likely to be exposed to the loneliness and hopelessness which ineluctably confront the last to be held within an eclipsed tradition. The present structure of the population shows a spiral of decline which has not been checked. Demoralization has become a feature of this spiral, accelerating it and then being accelerated by it. Population decline and depression among the people have become elements in a single and unremitting process.

Yet population decline cannot explain rejection of rural Irish life itself. Rather, the spiral has been set into its fastest motion *by* a rejection of rural life. The decline has not been halted, and is unlikely to be halted in the near future, precisely because country girls have refused to marry into local farms.* So long as they reject life in the parish, no new generation can emerge and no check to the downward trend can be effected. The sheer dearth of population creates real problems: community cohesion, defence against eroding doubt and intrusive influences, cannot be sustained; every parishioner must concede that

*As early as 1935 the importance of the woman's attitude to country life was noted: 'Few persons realize how much the stagnation of the country villages is a woman's question. Without their help every remedy is foredoomed to failure. From most, if not all, country activities women had dropped out. ... Without these interests rural life loses its zest: it becomes monotonous; it resolves itself into the struggle to make two ends meet on narrow incomes and the converging round of household duties.' Lord Ernle, *The Land and its People*, 1935, quoted by E. W. Martin (ed.), *Country Life in England*, London, 1949, p. 189.

They loaded the day-scoured implements on the cart
As the shadows of poplars crookened the furrows.
It was the evening, evening. Patrick was forgetting to be lonely
As he used to be in Aprils long ago.
It was the menopause, the misery-pause.

Patrick Kavanagh: *The Great Hunger*

somewhere, somehow, the traditional forms and forces of his community have gone wrong; the community is without its sense of integrity, while the individual is without his communally defined and accepted place. But these are all partly correlates and partly by-products of a process which has its root in an earlier break in the continuity of Irish life since the 1850s. That break came with and has been maintained by the disaffection which the young have come to feel for life at home on the land.

And as the 1950s advanced, the opportunities – social, financial and sexual – with which urban life tends to be identified were forced deeper and deeper into the consciousness of the community: tourists, the new films, television and ever glossier magazines brought their message into every country home.* The consequence was that Inishkillane began to feel itself to be a peripheral part of a single culture. More important, it began to see the relative disadvantage and inadequacy in traditional rural life. It was the girls of the parish who came more quickly and implacably to feel the disadvantages of staying in the countryside. The huge number of country girls in Irish towns and cities,

* The *Limerick Rural Survey* noted in 1962: 'Through the cinema and the radio, and above all by direct experience, either personal or through relatives, people in such conditions are ... becoming aware of the contrast between their way of life and that in other countries, especially in urban centres.... They are gradually becoming less willing to accept the frugal standards of previous generations' (p. 260).

working in any niche they can find, indicates how widespread this disaffection rapidly became. The girls' reaction has been more rapid and more determined, but now the men are following. And this reassessment of country life does not have its foundations in either demography or migration statistics alone.

Twelve of the 231 households in Inishkillane contain people suffering from mental illness associated with isolation and its concomitant depression. The nurse who comes each week to the small surgery at the back of a village bar claims that she dispenses more anti-depressants than headache tablets. Suicides, though carefully concealed in a Roman Catholic society wherever possible, are not rare. At least three have occurred in the parish over the past four years. The 'mental breakdown' is becoming almost a routine part of the country life. Typically, the 'mental breakdown' involves rapid and unpredictable alternation between a sobbing withdrawal and destruction of household property. As in the case of Joseph Murphy, it is invariably part of a life of ever-deepening and more hopeless isolation.

Joseph Murphy was born in 1915. The Murphy family farm is at the northern edge of Inishkillane, in a townland close to the sea. The old house where Joseph spent his childhood was built in the 1870s in strictly traditional style: its two rooms and loft were roofed with rush thatch. The building was sited in the shelter of a hollow at the foot of steep hills. The best fields on the thirty-acre farm were between the house and the seashore. Behind the house and up the hillside lay areas of rough grazing.

This farm supported a family of eight. Joseph is the youngest of six children. The oldest child in the family was born in 1905. Joseph had three sisters and two brothers. He remembers his childhood as a time of plenty: though the fare was not elaborate, there was food enough from the land for all of them. The farm grew fine crops of potatoes; three or four cows always provided milk and butter. Joseph's father went once to England and once to Scotland for work, but never stayed more than a few months.

On the whole he seems to have managed well enough without leaving County Clare. Joseph says he can remember a *poteen* still hidden in the high land behind the house. It may be that rents were paid with the help of a small whisky trade. But the family lived mainly off the land. If they received money from earlier generations of emigrants, Joseph never knew it.

In 1930, at the age of twenty-five, the oldest son Patrick emigrated to Chicago. Two years earlier the second oldest brother had been drowned. The reason Patrick gave for leaving was his loneliness after the death of his brother. 'And he's lonely after him still.' Then the oldest sister went to England, and was soon married there. The next sister followed her oldest brother to Chicago. By 1937 Joseph and his youngest sister were the last children at home.

From time to time Patrick wrote to his father suggesting that Joseph come and join him in America. He offered to pay the cost of the journey as well as to see Joseph safely into a good job. But Joseph was badly needed at home. He and his father were part of a seine crew. The land had to be worked. With the coming of the Land Commission the Murphy farm received a share in a hundred acres of rough grazing. More important, they were entitled to a grant towards building a new house. Joseph and his father planned to do the building themselves. And the father was hardly likely to encourage the last man in the Murphy line to leave the family farm. So the call to Chicago was ignored, and when the Murphys abandoned seine fishing in 1938 they promptly began work on their new home.

The house was built much closer to the road. It is large and solid, with two upstairs bedrooms, a spacious parlour and a kitchen. It has both electricity and running water. The two men built a garden on the slope of the land, and sited the building to give views over the sea. The roof is built with heavy squared rafters and slates. The old house has been turned into a cow-shed.

Invitations are not by printed card; indeed, formal invitations are not issued. The very wind for some days ahead seems to bear the news of a big night at So-and-so's. Thus, the boys and girls, and many not so young, come in on Saturday night after their labours in the fields and in the home. None is excluded – not the stranger, certainly, if he should chance that way.

A. P. Swann: *Romantic Inishowen*

By 1939 Joseph, his father and mother, and his sister Kathleen had moved into the new family home. The move was, as Joseph recalls, a time of great celebration for his parents. There were many 'big nights' in the new house before it had been occupied a full year. But Kathleen was not content. She was twenty-two and forever talking of leaving for America. Eventually she went to Dublin, worked in a hotel and finally made her way to England to join her married sister already there. So Joseph was the last child at home, a young man in a large new house on a comparatively good farm, living with his parents.

But Joseph's father was ageing. He had married at thirty-eight. His own father had died before agreeing to hand over the farm. At the time they were completing the new house Joseph's father was seventy-two. Two years later he died. At twenty-six Joseph was left alone in the house with his sixty-year-old mother. A generation earlier the death would have been followed by a marriage. Joseph was by traditional standards a very eligible bachelor. By 1941, however, there were too many eligible bachelors in Inishkillane. Joseph insists that his mother discouraged any matchmaking, argued that there was time enough for weddings and new families, pointed out that many a good man made no haste to marriage at forty. Either Joseph did not enter the competition for the girls who were ready to marry locally, or his endeavours met with failure. But by the time he had reached forty, in 1955, it was indeed unlikely that he would

... Maguire grunts and spits
Through a clay-wattled moustache and stares about him from the
*   height.*
His dream changes again like the cloud-swung wind
And he is not so sure now if his mother was right
When she praised the man who made a field his bride.
                        Patrick Kavanagh: *The Great Hunger*

find a bride at all in Inishkillane. The time for haste was long past.

In the summer of 1963 Joseph's mother died. She was eighty-two, and had been more or less bedridden for a year. His mother's death made Joseph acutely unhappy. His isolation seemed to him to have been completed. Around him the parish was dwindling; emigration had decimated his own generation; his loneliness was continually aggravated by the atrophied social life of the community. One of Joseph's sisters came home shortly after the funeral. It would appear that Joseph hoped she would offer to take him to England with her. But either she did not offer or when faced with the prospect of such complete change he refused. He does not like leaving the parish in any event, and is made uneasy even by the short journeys he occasionally makes to a town thirty miles away. Certainly Joseph became resigned to staying at home.

In 1964, scarcely a year after his mother's death, Joseph had a 'breakdown'. The details of the symptoms are unclear, but he was unable to sleep, kept bursting into tears, and confided to a cousin that he was intent on killing himself. The cousin spoke to the priest, the priest spoke to the doctor, and Joseph spent two months in hospital. After coming back to the house Joseph continued farming as he and his family had done for many decades. He kept only two cows, but still fattened a few cattle for marketing, grew potatoes and some green vegetables, saw to the hay for winter feed, cut turf, and tended half a dozen hens. He has all the skills to provide for his immediate needs, can churn butter, and bakes delicious bread. But the loneliness became more rather than less troublesome. Joseph stopped going to bed in his room upstairs, preferring to doze in a chair by the range. He sat on newspapers and pulled a blanket over his shoulders for warmth. The fewness of neighbours, the lack of neighbourliness itself, caused him long, despairing evenings.

Loneliness and breakdown proceeded in close partnership. After the first breakdown Joseph was reluctant to go into the village bars. He felt that local people thought him mad and feared him. Few as those visits to the bars had been before his hospitalization, they now became rare indeed. And the lack of visitors was reinterpreted: he came to believe that his neighbours did not like to visit him because he was 'not right in the head'. Illness compounded anxiety.

Soon after leaving hospital Joseph took a job as gardener to a local dispossessed landowner who had lost his estates but retained the family house and gardens. These gardens lie only three miles from the Murphy farm. Each morning Joseph cycled there, and spent four or five hours on the most menial parts of a gardener's work: sweeping and raking leaves, trimming overgrown beech hedges, cleaning the employer's cars. And Joseph Murphy was the only gardener. His hours at work were usually as solitary as his evenings at home. He had a minimum of contact with his employer. He rarely had any contact with the couple who worked in the employer's house. After work he came home to the farm, to milking and feeding the cows, as well as seeing to his dinner.

In 1968 came another breakdown. I was present for the first three days of Joseph's distress. At seven o'clock one morning he began forcing himself to vomit. Straining every muscle in his diaphragm he sank to his knees by the chair in which he had spent a sleepless night. He pulled an old newspaper from the range side, placed it to catch the few gobs of mucus and bile which ran off his chin. The effort forced tears to his eyes. The crisis had been precipitated by local opposition to Joseph's intention of selling part of his land to strangers.

The plot, on which the strangers planned to build a holiday home, was close to a village. Some of the villagers felt uneasy about the development. A shopkeeper-hotelier from the next parish led the opposition. Joseph assured this shopkeeper that the buyers had no intention of setting up any competition, had no wish to start either guest house or shop. But the shopkeeper insisted that he should be offered the land before any outsider, and that in any case he was certainly willing to pay more for it. The shopkeeper asked the parish priest to represent the local opposition to Joseph's selling to outsiders. The priest agreed that the land should be sold to the highest bidder, and therefore agreed that Joseph should sell to a local bidder if the best bid was local. The shopkeeper insisted that his was the best bid. The priest went to Joseph and argued the shopkeeper's case.

The priest went to the Murphy house on a Monday evening. Joseph was immediately disturbed by the visit. It represented the most official opposition to his plans, and gave the situation an intimidating seriousness. He wanted to sell to the strangers. He felt that in them he would have new friends in the district. He was enthusiastic about helping them do the building work and making sure everything was 'in order' when they were away. It would have been a place for Joseph to visit any evening he felt inclined. They would have bought milk and eggs from him perhaps, and come to his house to collect them. He would for at least part of the year have been drawn into an almost familial situation. The chance for another hundred pounds in no way made Joseph prefer the shopkeeper's bid. But the apparent intensity of local opinion frightened him out of selling to his new friends.

The vomiting was followed by bursts of choking sobs. Then

Joseph rushed out of the house, turned towards the sea, and shouted his determination to drown himself. Eventually he slumped down in his chair by the range, and for several hours sat quietly, occasionally calling out his despair and breaking into brief but convulsive weeping.

The following day Joseph's condition had deteriorated. His despair had become more violent. Although he had by this time slept but a few hours in three days and eaten only mouthfuls of bread, Joseph periodically took hold of objects in his kitchen and smashed them on the floor. His cousin Cornelius, who had come to visit and found Joseph in the middle of this crisis, had difficulty in restraining him by force. Later in the afternoon Cornelius went to the village, confronted the shopkeeper, and asked him why he so firmly insisted on buying the land. The shopkeeper repeated his earlier statements: the land must go to the highest bidder; whatever any outsider bid, he would better it. Cornelius returned to Joseph that evening, and they talked of the shopkeeper's adamant attitude. Only by violating the most fundamental rule of selling could Joseph imagine escaping the trap.

At the end of this conversation Joseph once again became hysterical. He began calling for his mother, asking her to come back and help him. Once more he ran from the house, shouting that it was time to drown himself. But Joseph allowed Cornelius to bring him inside again. As he sat down in his chair sobbing, Joseph began shouting reproaches against his mother for ever having left him alone at all. Suddenly he jumped up and rushed into the other ground floor room, where the family's best furniture and most valued possessions were kept undisturbed. He began breaking a chair. Then he virtually slid onto the floor, and squatted with his back leaning against the wall. Bowing his head, exhausted and sobbing, Joseph began pounding his fists on the floor and calling for his mother. His position, gestures, his tone and words, were all those of a child of five or six. Soon after this he returned to his chair: the worst seemed to have passed. It was mostly because of his cousin's help and encouragement that Joseph was not hospitalized.

I last saw Joseph Murphy in January of 1971. He had stopped working as a gardener. The job was taken by a young man of twenty-three who lived alone with his father on the other side of the parish. Joseph was still negotiating with the shopkeeper for the sale of his building plot. He had not suffered any more emotional illness, but his sense of isolation was unabated. He complained that community life was quieter than ever. 'I'll be like that Sonny Liston,' Joseph remarked, 'I'll be dead two weeks before anyone about here'll come to the house and find me.'

The contractions and decline described in Chapters 1 and 2 have all taken place in Inishkillane. Situated in a landscape of astonishing beauty, where the long evening light touches a succession of different colours and shades across the hills and mountains, it is all the same a sad place for most of the year. The parish schoolteacher believes that the future will bring mechanization to the few best farms and tourist facilities to the more enterprising households. The priest is more pessimistic, and sees only an irreversible decline of everything, including all

---

The death of the Charlestowns of the West was not the brutal death of the head-on car smash: if it had that brutal fate we might have been galvanized into action.

It is hard to see death when it is disguised and tricked out in the surface trappings of life. Those parents kept the homes open and the postman kept them in touch with their sons and daughters. The cheques and money orders kept on coming, the sons and daughters came home faithfully every August and every Christmas.

James N. Healy: *The Death of an Irish Town*

---

farming. The statistics suggest that very few people will be in the parish in twenty years. Perhaps the tourist industry will continue expanding, and will maintain a few families in the countryside. But there are no children in Inishkillane under school age. The pattern of traditional community and the distinctive farming it has sustained have been ascendent since the last disaster in rural Ireland, which had run its course by 1852. This life in Inishkillane is finally expiring.

4 Family Life

The traditional Irish home was to all appearances uncompromisingly patriarchal. The farmer-father was in all important matters the final arbiter and judge: he made all decisions about the land; he conducted all deals at the markets; he negotiated his children's marriages and dowries.

The dominance which the father had over his sons has been a source of amazement to most commentators on Irish life. Arensberg and Kimball describe how a father at the fair would not allow his full-grown sons to handle any part of the dealings or even have money in their possession at all.* They also relate how the Land Commission, when employing local men in land reclamation and fencing, found that they often had to pay their employees' fathers: on payday the 'old fellows walk sometimes many miles to be paid the wages their sons have earned'.†

My father, after a few kingly turns back and forth the floor, to show everybody that he was lord and master in his own home, left, as was usual with him, the tinker to my mother's care, and saying to them, 'Let ye not feel strange...' stepped out and glanced hastily up and down the road, looking for new worlds to conquer. I, a boy of ten, stood by the wall, admiring his greatness.

Pat Mullen: *Come Another Day*

---

*Conrad M. Arensberg and Solon T. Kimball, *Family and Community in Ireland*, Harvard University Press, 1968, pp. 53–4.
†ibid., p. 54.

Arensberg and Kimball tell of an incident in the Irish Parliament which showed the father's lasting authority in his son's life: a deputy in the *Dáil* dropped into the country idiom and pleaded for special treatment in division for 'boys of 45 and older'.*

A son came under his father's full control only after confirmation. Before that his life did not go much beyond home and schooling, in both of which he was his mother's responsibility. The more intimate relationship, formed as it was before the boy was thirteen, was thus with the mother. Contact with the father was minimal, and entailed more discipline than companionship. Once at work on the farm, however, sons began to spend the greater part of every day in the father's company, working under his direction. Until a son married he remained in this subservient role. And marriage was a long time coming. The change in social and farming practice which occurred in the 1840s and 1850s therefore meant that the son who was waiting for the inheritance had to wait as a 'boy' for as much as twenty-five or thirty years. Such a system required an extraordinarily deep-felt respect for the father's authority.

The girls were not subject to the same delay and subservience. They lived always in a close and affective relationship with their mothers, which ended only with their marriage, usually at a relatively early age. But the girls did directly experience the patriarchal quality of country life in other ways. At marriage the bride moved to the groom's family home, taking nothing with her. Dowries were given by a girl's father to her new husband. The new wife owned not so much as a teacup. And she owned no more when she was eighty: everything passed to her son, whose wife in her turn would use but never own the household possessions. Women were also excluded from the social centres of the community: they never went to the bars, rarely exchanged visits, and only when they had reached old age was the wisdom attributed to years allowed to transcend, in public life, the

*ibid., p. 55.

insignificance attributed to womanhood. In home and community life alike, therefore, the woman's influence may have been significant, but it was informal and domestic: women had at least to appear to be without authority just as they were in practice without possessions.*

Although women in the traditional society were without any formal authority in family and home, they played a significant part in the struggle against landlords and agents. Synge and Mullen both described the women's angry resistance to rent-collectors, law-enforcers and bailiffs.† Lady Gregory in *Visions and Beliefs in the West of Ireland* records the use of magical power in support of the social struggle:

At childbirth ... some of the old women are able to put a part of the pain upon the man, or any man. There was a woman in labour near Ovon, and there were two policemen out walking that night, and one of them went into the home to light his pipe.... And no sooner was he there than he began to roar and catch hold of his belly and he fell down by the roadside roaring ...‡

But this part in the society's overall struggle did not seem to give Irish countrywomen any greater or more formal place in the daily life of their society.

Marriage in the traditional context was fundamentally un-romantic: arranged by a matchmaker, attended by endless negotiations and wranglings over dowry and worth, the wedding

---

*Obviously the effective influence of the woman varied from house to house. Claude Lévi-Strauss has put the general point well: 'But this is merely a social attitude. When a man and his woman are alone beside their fire he will listen to her complaints, take note of her wishes, and in his turn ask her help in a hundred-and-one little things; masculine braggadocio gives place to the collaboration of two partners who know very well that one cannot get along without the other' (*World on the Wane*, London, 1961, pp. 279–80).

†See especially J. M. Synge, *The Aran Islands*, London, 1921, and Pat Mullen, *Hero Breed*, Faber, 1936.

‡London, 1920, vol. 2, p. 26.

eventually paired a girl of twenty with a man often well over forty. But traditional family life also ensured that a couple, on marriage, did not enter a life of unrelenting and demanding proximity – proximity which an 'arranged' couple may well have found intolerable. Even the details of the division of labour between men and women in the home maintained a distance between them: the woman got up first in the morning to lay the fire and prepare the first cup of tea of the day. She then had to see to the children, feed them and make them ready for school. After that came milking. Meanwhile the husband had taken his breakfast and set out for the fields. He returned during the day for his dinner, which was prepared and served him by his wife: they did not sit at table together. The same applied to the tea in the evening. After the men had eaten, the wife fed the children and completed jobs about the house and yard. Typically, the husband would be out visiting neighbours or have some neighbours sitting with him at his own fireside. Husbands went to bed before their wives, who last thing each night would damp out the fire and prepare the kitchen for the morning. Husband and wife may have been alone together in bed but even then, with a large number of children in the small cottage, there was scarcely much privacy.* In such a context the social impact of the relationship was sure to be far more compelling than the personal.

Probably a couple saw more of each other at the *ceilidhes* and crossroads dances preceding their marriage than they did after the ceremony when the bride had moved to her husband's home. Of course marriage was a very real partnership, but for most of its span, with the home full of children and time taken up with farmwork or winter festivities, it consisted of co-operation without great physical closeness. Even in old age,

---

*In a two-room cottage with perhaps ten children, the parents usually shared their bed with the youngest children. More urbane couples would scarcely accept this situation.

Nora: *What way would I live, and I an old woman, if I didn't marry a man with a bit of a farm, and cows on it, and sheep on the back hills?*

Michael (nodding): *That's true, Nora, and maybe it's no fool you were, for there's good grazing on it, if it is a lonesome place, and I'm thinking it's a good sum he's left behind.*

J. M. Synge: *The Shadow of the Glen*

after retirement, couples still did not spend much time together: traditional activities, stemming as they did from a highly developed division of sexual roles, still kept them apart.

The kind of romance which matchmakers might appear to obviate or ignore had little relevance in that kind of marriage. No doubt a very real understanding between partners was able to flourish, and that understanding was exactly the thing which matchmakers could almost guarantee. The arranging, after all, insured that the closest attention was given to common interests of the most down-to-earth kind. So long as the rural communities were resilient and tightly integrated, the values and expectations of most people harmonized with the life-style they were offered. Strains and weaknesses in a system emerge as the popular consciousness is tempered and altered by internal dislocation or by information about other societies. In the traditional Irish farm family, these strains were contained for a surprisingly long period. Certainly, the traditional pattern of authority over the 'boy' of forty, and the displacement of the wife from the centres of influence as well as the burdensome role she was obliged to endure, was alive on the west coast of Ireland well into the 1930s. The endurance of this system is all the more remarkable since this particular order of family life established itself quite suddenly around the time of the Great Famine. Prior to that, sub-division and early marriage must have

given a quite different structure and tenor to family relationships.

One strain which did not go unremarked by the country
people themselves, however, was in the awkward and frequently
stressful relationship between the new young wife and the
mother-in-law. Just as marriage ensured a separation between
husband and wife, by the same token it thrust the two women
in the house into constant interaction. Between wife and mother-
in-law the authority was inevitably uncertain. The older woman
was likely to accept the presence of a new woman, so young but
so important, only with reluctance; the wife was inevitably
anxious about the situation, and quick to see advice and suggestions as interference and bullying. It is highly significant
that the Gaelic for a new bride is 'cliaban isteach', which literally
translates as 'relation coming in'.* Yet despite this particular
source of friction the traditional farm family appears to have
been harmonious. The endless round of work and the highly
convivial society no doubt helped defuse and minimize stress
points in the home and tensions in the community.

The architecture of the traditional home also cushioned
possible awkwardness between the new family and the old
couple. With some regional variation, houses built in the last
half of the nineteenth century are what people today refer to as
a traditional Irish cottage. This cottage was extremely simple
and in many ways excellently suited to the terrain: constructed
directly on the earth from rough stone, and roofed with rush
and straw thatch on a frame of beams and branches, it could be
built relatively quickly and cheaply from local materials. With
annual thatching and whitewashing these homes could be kept
dry and warm. The ground plan was simple: a large kitchen, a

* In fact 'cliaban' can be used to mean any relation by marriage. A
County Kerry man who spoke very little Irish once assured me that
when a bride was referred to as 'cliaban isteach' the strict meaning was
'stranger coming in'.

small room at the west end of the house, and a loft created by a platform built under the kitchen roof.* The older children slept on this platform, while the parents, and the younger children slept in the kitchen. The west room was for the retired couple. In this way the new and the old part of the family were formally divided, and the old people were guaranteed some privacy in a very public home.

This family life, with all its details and idiosyncrasies, is evoked by Maurice O'Sullivan, Peig Sayers, Peadar O'Donnell and Synge in their reminiscences of life in the west. Arensberg and Kimball carefully documented the division of labour, the daily routine and the inter-personal relationships in the County Clare families they observed in the 1930s. And what they have to say of Clare certainly applies to the farm families throughout the western seaboard at the same period. In all the literature, just as in the stories and recollections of the older people today, these families are characterized as outwardly rigidly patriarchal, with a woman's subtle influence exercised outside

---

> Maguire was faithful to death;
> He stayed with his mother till she died
> At the age of ninety-one.
> She stayed too long,
> Wife and mother in one.
> When she died
> The knuckle-bones were cutting the skin of her son's backside
> And he was sixty-five.
>
> Patrick Kavanagh: *The Great Hunger*

---

*There is considerable regional variation in Irish cottages and the history of their development offers some insight into the course of rural development. See E. Estyn Evans, *Irish Heritage* (Dundalk, 1949), and F. H. A. Aalen's discussion of Donegal cottages in F. H. A. Aalen and Hugh Brody, *Gola: The Life and Last Days of an Island Community*, Cork: Mercier, 1969.

the principal arenas of community life. Under the unquestionable authority of fathers, sons endured protracted 'boyhood'. Children were brought up with unremitting strictness, and accepted their position in the family and community. This passivity of the younger generation is surprising for the degree in which it endured the successive waves of emigration that were an inevitable by-product of the system. But this traditional family could survive only so long as the children allowed it to: with the possibility of emigration ever present, no one was forced to wait or marry or so much as help on the land. Parents eventually came to depend on an appeal to duty alone. The many decades in which this appeal succeeded give a measure of how deeply the traditional family etched its roles and hierarchies into the consciousness of each generation.

In the summer of 1968 I went with a group of young men to the Inishkillane bog. Three of the men were brothers, and two of the brothers were barmen returned from England to spend a few weeks on the family farm, helping and visiting and enjoying the tourist season in local bars. The third brother was the youngest, and at eighteen had begun to reconcile himself to staying at home and looking after his parents in their old age. The other man was a neighbour who was hiring them a tractor and trailer to draw the load. The family hiring the tractor was very poor. They kept three cows and lived for the most part on money which emigrants in the family sent somewhat irregularly out of their earnings abroad. Both brothers in the family had brought from England a present of money for the parents.

The work was simple: turf had been dried and stacked by the lane leading into the bog, and all we had to do was throw the sods into the cart. After a few hours the cart was heaped full, and with the sun just beginning to set, we drove the five miles back to the house. The three brothers and I were perched rather precariously on top of the load while the tractor owner was driving. The route back followed a tiny winding lane, and the cart rocked wildly at each bend. It seemed to be the rocking which precipitated the first gusts of hilarity.

Hilarity was initially expressed by the screaming of jokes at other carts – for the most part horse-drawn – which we overtook on the way. But soon the brothers began to hurl turf at the hedgerows, seeing just how far each could throw despite the rocking and shaking of the cart. This throwing gradually turned into something more directly aggressive: they began to throw sods at drivers of the carts we overtook. Each time a hit was scored or a sod tumbled noisily into the vicinity of driver and horse, the brothers screamed with laughter. They also yelled jokes and insults at the men, who waved angry fists at us as we noisily passed. As the journey continued the throwing and shouting became wilder and wilder, until there was a more or less continuous shower of turf spraying from our load and the noise of laughter and shouting must have echoed far into the quiet evening countryside.

The loss of turf over the whole journey was neither great nor serious: the load was enormous, and turf is hardly a scarcity in the west of Ireland. But there seemed a special significance in the scene: the young men who had managed to introduce some mechanization into their work, hurling the very symbol of Irish country life with utter abandon and considerable aggression at those more staid and traditional, and at the very fields themselves.

As we eventually came into the village, the lane narrowed and twisted between the houses. At many of these twists the cart almost scraped the houses closest to the roadside. And as we edged past them, the top of our load was almost exactly level with the edges of the rush thatch. Suddenly the oldest brother pulled out a small pocket knife and began to slash at the bindings which held thatch to the branch rafters. His gesture was not humorous, and all of us on the cart were aware of tension – a tension which seemed to have its source deep within him – as he swung the knife wildly at each string we swayed past. He cut only a few of them, for the most part the difficulties created by our movements and the toughness of the bindings defeated him. Soon we arrived at their house, and the load was piled into the yard.

As soon as we had finished heaping the load against the byre, we all went into the house for tea. It was a completely traditional house – two rooms on the ground floor, a small loft for the children under the kitchen roof. On the table the old mother had prepared a plate of bread, and a pot of tea stood ready. The father was sitting taking his tea at the table. It is customary for visitors to sit and eat with the father and the working men, and the mother waved me to a seat at the table. But the second oldest brother caught at my arm and said: 'Come and sit over by the fire, don't take any notice of them.' He laughed as he said this, and began to tell me how stupid his parents were, how they didn't know anything, being so old-fashioned. I insisted that I should sit with the parents, but the mother suddenly agreed with her son and said yes, it would be much more interesting for me to sit with the boys around the fire. So she brought tea to us there. Throughout these exchanges the father said nothing at all. He kept on eating his tea, occasionally smiling in our direction. The sons completely ignored him.

The parents did not appear to find their children's behaviour particularly objectionable or offensive. Whatever the brothers asked for was given them, and the two older ones maintained throughout tea and conversation a domineering and disparaging manner. Yet there were moments when the mother seemed actually proud of her sons. She kept telling me what they did and how well they had fared in England, never for a moment reacting against the way they greeted everything she said with a studied indifference. The youngest was the quietest, but he was obviously impressed by his brothers' 'style', and sought to emulate it when he did speak. As the parental acqui-

*The children also develop a tolerant or openly malicious contempt
for their parents as stupid, unknowing of American ways, con-
cerning which the children regard themselves as authorities. By and
large the parents are obstacles to be avoided or circumvented whenever possible. And while the resulting lack of identification with the
parents virtually obviates demonstrations of affection, it also saves
the children from feelings of guilt and repressed hostility.*

A. W. Green: *The Middle-Class Male Child and Neurosis*

escence in this aggressive behaviour became more and more
evident, my original embarrassment subsided. It became
obvious that in the relationships between the parents and
children of the family, the behaviour and attitudes I was
witnessing were accepted. It was certainly a far cry from the
traditional farm family. The father either approved of or was
ambivalent about his sons' behaviour.

Country men who today have sons of twenty must themselves have been faced with the chance of emigration. Many of
them did spend some time abroad or were part of seasonal
migrations to work on construction sites and farms in England
and Scotland. Their own brothers and sisters left the countryside and sent news of the success they had achieved away from
home. Perhaps many of these fathers of today deeply regret that
they did not emigrate themselves. In any case, there can be very
few men in the Irish countryside who wholeheartedly endorse
the contemporary rural way of life, who unambiguously value
it above emigration. Just as they faced a choice between staying
and leaving thirty years before, so they now have ambivalence
about their sons' attitudes and behaviour.

In Connemara I once worked for several days with a middle-
aged farmer who maintains a little over forty acres. The work
was slow and painstaking: we were making haystacks, one man

standing on the growing heap, binding each armful of hay into the pile, while the other handed up the armfuls to him. When the stack had been carefully built in this way, it had to be secured with ropes crisscrossed individually over the top and weighted with stones. Under these ropes a careful topping of rush thatch was laid. In this way the small stack could be secured against the long months of hard weather which sweep the countryside through winter and spring. At the end of the first day's work the man suddenly told me that he was surprised that I should be willing to help. I told him I enjoyed it, and his surprise increased. He told me that his sons, two of whom were in the house, refused to do the work. 'They won't do anything that's not machines and tractors and cars.' After he said this there was a long silence. I had no reply to make. The man broke the silence: 'They're right. They're too clever for this sort of thing.'

So the fathers share some of their son's rejection of country life. They are aware of the relative disadvantage which many of the sons feel staying on the land must bring. And around the fathers stand the mute testimonies to the failure which seems to have stricken traditional country life and farm family: empty houses, declining communities, and the painfully large number of farms where a man well beyond the marrying age lives on in deepening isolation. The rapid disintegration of life in the west of Ireland has been taking a most drastic and profound toll in the past thirty years – the period during which the fathers of today's younger emigrants have been watching the next generation grow up in their own homes. These fathers can see what the future would hold for a young man staying on the farm. They are aware that the young women are leaving, that marriage is becoming less and less possible for farmers' sons. Informed by that awareness, it is unlikely that the fathers could unequivocally expect their own sons to stay on the land.*

* In their discussion of parent–child relationships among the Polish

But to this source of uncertainty and ambivalence must be added the far more material way in which the authority of the father has been undermined and displaced. Traditionally the father owned the single most important source of livelihood – the family farm. Gradually, however, that has been rivalled and in many instances supplanted by another source: money from abroad.* This money is essential to farm families, and it is in large part earned by the sons. Of course this contribution by the emigrant is by no means new. But in the past few decades, with more produce being bought, fewer men to work the land, and much more elaborate expectations even among the most rural families, the remittance has assumed far greater significance. In purely economic terms, the sons of farm families in the remoter and poorer regions of the west have a central position.

In summer it is possible to watch young men who have come home for a week or two's holiday boasting of their earning power in England. They recount their importance, their speed of promotion, and they substantiate these tales with wads of pound notes. Parents complain that children do not send the remittance the way they used to. By this parents mean that their

---

peasantry, W. I. Thomas and F. Znaniecki suggest that traditional familism explains leniency: 'Parents are curiously *tolerant* – show a remarkable leniency toward the young generation and a sympathetic interest in ambitions and pleasures which they do not share personally – an interest which is explained by that conversion of personal into familial aspirations which, as one knows, usually follows the social maturity of the peasant' (*The Polish Peasant in Europe and America*, New York, 1927, p. 1199). In Ireland family relationships have been changed by the forces which have weakened familism itself. Cf. A. C. MacIntyre: 'The impact of industrialism and of a liberal and individualist ethos destroys this conception of human relationships in terms of roles and functions' (*Social and Moral Change*, Oxford, 1967, p. 72).

*Welfare payments have also supplemented cash earnings, but fathers benefit from them as much as their sons.

children are not putting a few shillings in the post each week and dutifully sending it home. But many of the girls continue the practice and those shillings have often become a pound or two, while sons, many of whom are as concerned with impressing their peers as with subsidizing the families, often prefer to appear at Christmas and mid-summer with an impressively fat 'roll'. In this way the irregular but much larger gift has partially replaced the regular remittance. It is very unlikely that the average income per household from remittances has declined.*

In most villages there is an inexhaustible gossip surrounding remittances. People are forever calculating how much a particular family is receiving from which children, and every time anyone makes a grand purchase, a dozen rumours spread about who sent money when. Certainly, many farm families do seem to have money for buying the things they need, and often families doing the buying are conspicuously without much source of income of their own. In a bar in West Clare I noticed that many of the men who drank most came from very poor homes. With some difficulty created by their unbelievable generosity I tried to count how much beer the men were drinking each day. Totals were impressive: several of the heavier drinkers were consuming between ten and fifteen pints of Guinness and a whisky or two in between. If this rate was maintained five days each week for the eight weeks of the tourist season, expenditure on drink alone for each must have been no less than £70, and probably was a good deal more. For a small farm in the west of Ireland, that kind of expenditure is not possible without the help of the remittance. Seventy pounds is more than the average farm is able to earn per year from its marketed produce.

*In 1958 remittances constituted approximately 2·5 per cent of Ireland's national income. Between 1958 and 1964 this percentage fell slightly, but the absolute monetary value of remittances increased from £12 million to £13 million. See David O'Mahoney, *The Irish Economy, An Introductory Description*, Cork, 1967, pp. 157 ff.

The authority of parents is thus undermined by their dimin-
ished importance in the household economy. But parents also
feel vulnerable before their children today in a way that they
never had reason to fear before. If the last son leaves, they are
going to be left isolated. Around them are precedents which
can only keep feeding their fears. To keep the last son they
must appeal to his sense of duty and pity. But they are ambivalent in their own feelings about that duty, are uncertain about
the son's advantage. So, in the last resort, parents must ask a
son to do the thing they might have almost refused to do themselves thirty years before, the thing which part of them feels is
not in their son's own best interests. This fear and all the con-
fusions which attend it can produce a persistent and debilitating
anxiety in parents. They are people for the most part un-
accustomed to discussing such matters, and instead watch
quietly and tensely their children's every move.

John Joyce was a last son in his family. The situation had
been worsened by the sudden early death of his father. He lived
alone with his mother in a tiny village in County Cork. John
had never had a job, and the farm consisted of only two small
fields immediately adjacent to the house. He insisted that he
suffered from a bad stomach and succeeded in collecting sickness benefits every week. Outwardly at least, John was a perfectly healthy man of twenty-two. The family received some
money from another son and a daughter who both worked in
London.

John drank heavily in the summer weeks, and drove a very
old black Morris Minor. Every time John refused to do anything his mother began shouting at him, saying what a terrible
son he was and how she'd be better off without him to feed
every day. At the climax of every such argument John would
declare that he was off and going to England and would not be
back in a good while. And every time he made the threat his
mother said: 'You wouldn't do that, and leave me here on my

own, with nobody to help me out.' At this John always walked out of the house, got into his car and accelerating noisily drove off towards the nearby town. Several times I met his mother standing outside the house looking down the road, seeing if there was any sign of John's black car. When I spoke to her, she asked me had I seen him 'in town', was he drinking in the bars, did I think he had taken off to England.

The woman was always desperate with worry when John was away from the house, continually fidgeting and asking over and over if it was likely that her son had gone away to England. On one occasion she asked him to go and buy some meat at the butcher's in town, and when John had been away an hour longer than she'd expected, she began declaring that he had 'buggered off to England and won't be coming back to me'. And when he did return, many hours later, very drunk but in good humour, she cursed him roundly for staying away and frightening her so.

John Joyce is perhaps an extreme case, and his mother's fears both more developed and more openly expressed than most. But her predicament and most of what she feels about it are typical enough. Moreover, the sons who stay (like the sons who visit) *are* very helpful, even if they have an extraordinary supremacy in the family, and even if the parents cannot unambiguously feel entitled to ask them to stay at home. Without John, Mrs Joyce could not have kept two cows, nor could she have taken an adequate crop of hay from her two fields. Perhaps more important, she would have had to buy turf or some alternative expensive fuel. Even apart from the fear of loneliness, her need for John was real.

On a family farm, where far more people must be fed and far more land cultivated, the need for additional labour becomes dire. All the most important work on these small farms is slow; machinery is hardly used at all. In Connemara I have helped harvest oats by sickle. Milking is by hand, and to prepare lazy-beds in the hard shallow ground requires extraordinary stamina and patience. The help of a sturdy school-leaver is invaluable.

Just as the older farmers of today feel more keenly the need for help, so the sons who do work at home are given much greater responsibility. Patrick Lynch, for example, comes home to County Kerry for lobster fishing and haymaking in the summer. He likes to be in Ireland for those months ('When I'm hearing that cuckoo in England, I can't stay working over there'), but is always glad to go back to England in the autumn ('The old place is too lonesome in the wintertime, and the money to be made in London'). Patrick is the last child in his family to spend any time at home: during the winter months, when he is away, the parents are alone in their cottage. During his stay, Patrick works long hours every day, maintaining the farm and supplementing the earnings in whatever way he can. But most important, when Patrick is home he does all the buying and selling of cattle for the year. He goes every two weeks to the local fair, taking the stock he wants to sell, and buying replacements. It is Patrick who makes all the decisions about the selling – picking out animals he thinks are ready to go, and negotiating prices he is prepared to accept. And it is Patrick who stands in the market street eyeing the stock others have brought in, and eventually selecting the animals he wants to buy. Occasionally his father goes into town to the fair with him, but even then Patrick handles both money and decisions.

Patrick is a bachelor of twenty-six. When I asked his father if he thought the boy good at buying and selling, I was told: 'Those buyers from Dublin are hard men. It's not the way they used to be. Paddy can talk to those men and they're after understanding him.' The father is no longer likely to go and collect his son's wages. Their roles have been altered and in some measure even reversed. Areas of competence have been freshly conceived. Sons quickly cease to be 'boys' in the west of Ireland today.

The daughters in farm families are as separated from their fathers today as they always have been. And since they only very rarely consider marriage to a local man, even that corner of parental authority has been eroded which was formerly implicit in negotiations and discussions between prospective partners' fathers. A daughter still does not eat at the same time as her father. She rarely has occasion to talk to him at all. As the traditional authority and established structure of family life have weakened, so fathers have become more and more remote from their daughters. This strange distance is often accompanied by real embarrassment on the daughters' part: I have often seen a girl giggle as her father left the kitchen, as if there was something a little absurd in his demeanour which could never be expressed in front of him. Such tiny signs are not easily interpreted, but it could be that the gulf between father and daughter, based as it is on a sense of the vast difference between their preoccupations and conceptions, necessarily includes an element of awe as its counterpart. That is to say, because the father represents the traditional milieu, he is 'old-fashioned' and therefore, in the terms of a modern girl, a bit 'peculiar'; in coming from that milieu he has expected an unrelaxing respect from his children. So daughters allow distance and separation of every kind and are silent in his presence, yet titter as he leaves the room. Certainly the gulf between father and daughter is wide, and few children are emotionally able to cross it.

Between daughters and their mothers there are usually much

In a little while we met my two aunts. They tore me assunder with kisses, for women are the very devil for plamas.* *... Why wouldn't they take it fine and soft like a man? Not at all, they must be fawning on you every time they come across you.*

Maurice O'Sullivan: *Twenty Years A-Growing*

[* soft, coaxing talk]

surer bonds of sympathy. In many respects the strong relationship between mothers and daughters is continuous with the
tradition. But it was the women who first felt able to leave the
countryside. Mothers are even better able to sympathize with
their daughters' desire to emigrate than fathers with their sons'.
Moreover, the woman's role and status in the social structure
have, ironically enough, given her an emotional freedom to
bring the most drastic change of all to the communities. Having
no part in any inheritance, the woman has always been without
any material possessions. Sons inherited the house, the very
cups and saucers in it, and the land. But with the inheritance
went duty and responsibility: they were to keep it intact, and
to maintain for generations to come the land that had for
generations past been in the family. Only with considerable
difficulty – as testified by a multitude of isolated bachelors
living on the land – could a son, the owner and inheritor, defy
his duty and neglect his responsibility. Even the last daughter,
however, has been spared this tension, and has felt free to leave
home without guilt.

The girls who come home to rural Ireland for their holidays
often laugh and joke with their mothers about a farm woman's
onerous life. But the visiting emigrant often has an ascendency
which is less charming. Ann Kenny returned to her home in
Inishkillane after being away nine years in America. Her parents
went by taxi from their home village to meet her off the plane
at Shannon. With them they took relatives from the neighbourhood – four of Ann's cousins, an uncle, an aunt, and the ageing
grandmother. It is customary for a family group to meet the
returning emigrant. Ann Kenny's first words to her mother on
arrival were: 'Did you have to bring half the village?' Then,
on arriving back at her family home, she asked her mother to
take down all the old religious pictures and calendars off the
walls. Her mother complied. And Ann insisted on going out
drinking in the bar in the evenings.

With the son selling cattle at the fair and a daughter out drinking in the bar, traditional family life is overthrown. And the new ascendancy of the young does not lead only to the bar or the fair, but to city life beyond them. For the most part, country girls do not go out drinking, and the fair is a periodic interruption to a long quiet year. Despite its new set of relationships, the family is much quieter and more private than ever before. The highly developed sense of privacy is outlined later. The atrophy of community life which it accompanies has already been described, and that too has altered the quality of family life on the countryside farms.

Reduction in community life and the insularity of each household has also changed the quality of marriage. Traditionally the couple on marrying entered into co-operation without much intimacy. Husband and wife were rarely alone, and always busy with their own sphere of activities. But with the contraction of these activities and the general atrophy in social conditions, marriage has come to involve much more proximity. With not much work on the land, very little social life in the villages, and rarely much rationale for visiting, husband and wife are together in the house for much of the time. A system which had evolved in a traditional society in response to very specific sets of social and economic needs could not easily support that kind of change.

Conditions of isolation and privacy require a romantic conception and prelude to marriage. Alongside the new social conditions within which marriage must now take place, a greater consciousness of urban ways and attitudes has also developed. This consciousness includes a far clearer idea of what the romance in marriage is supposed to be. Indirectly, it is from films, magazines and newspapers that the women of rural Ireland have drawn these romantic conceptions. In a situation where loneliness and isolation were beginning to abound, these ideas were sure to take a firm root, but they can not be realized in that

Danny: *The meadow'll do to be done tomorrow. Why don't you let me do what's to be done in the home, an' you go 'n mow the meadow? Why don't you do that? Don't you do that? You do that? Agony to look at you; agony to listen to you; agony, agony, to be anywhere near you.*

Lizzie: *I'd just like to see you doin' what's to be done about the home – I'd just like to see you.*

Danny: *What is there to be done about the home – will you tell us that?*

Lizzie: *There's the pig 'n the heifer 'n the hens to be fed 'n tended. There's ironing, cooking, washing 'n sewing to be done.*

Sean O'Casey: *The End of the Beginning*

situation. For the girls at least this means yet another displacement and potential source of anxiety. So women go to the cities to marry and raise families. To a majority of the generation of young women just leaving school and deciding their futures, the prospect of marriage in the countryside is too absurd to consider. They go to dances when they come home for visits, but mock the incompetence of the young men and do not take seriously any proposals which might entail a life in rural Ireland. These young women do not have the anxieties which seem to beset many of the young men, and they have a much clearer sense of how to appear sophisticatedly urban. They feel little duty towards traditional demands of country life, and can see no other reason for marrying locally.

Traditional family life pre-supposed a willingness on the part of young people to stay on the land. It also required a vigorous community to protect its women. Neither conditions are any longer fulfilled. The authority, status, and role structure have been undermined. The women will not tolerate the demands which farm life imposes on them. For the young man who is expected to inherit the family land this new situation creates a dilemma.* It has allowed the young woman a new consciousness of her predicament. Guilt-free emigration has become as natural as knowing what you want.

Today, the west room in many homes is used either as a bedroom for parents or a parlour for visitors. When it is used as a parlour the best furniture is put there with photographs of children who have emigrated. And in the newer houses, which have more rooms, there is also a small parlour leading off from the kitchen. These parlours celebrate the recent success of the family as the west room formerly symbolized the succession of generations. But the success of the family of today is indicated by pictures of the new generation making its life abroad, by signs of material prosperity imported from a very different culture: the nicely covered chair, perfect cleanliness, a small sideboard, the neat tablecloth. The parlour is rarely used by farm families. Visitors from among the tourists are led in there for tea. With so little use the parlour becomes more completely a symbol. It represents both the forces that have worked their changes on Irish family life and the absence of a generation for the future.

* In her account of a Welsh village Isabel Emmett cites another kind of difference between young men and young women's relationship to home: 'Men are more vulnerable to the appeal of the home (prestige) ladder because it usually contains an appeal to their masculinity. They were brought up to think it is manly to do manual work; from an early age they have heard strength praised as proof of manliness' (*A North Wales Village*, Routledge & Kegan Paul, 1964, p. 45).

5 Community and Co-operation

This lurking and sometimes intrusive presence of the past might perhaps be supposed to weaken or dull the impact of the present. The contrary is the case. This crowding in of history serves instead to intensify a consciousness of the pressures and contradictions of life and society in the present.

Claud Cockburn: *I Claud*

Self-reliance lies at the very heart of peasant life. At the edge of feudalism, with early capitalist development, and now in advanced industrial societies, alongside the most fundamental upheavals of history, peasant life has endured. The peasantry's remoteness from the socio-economic and cultural forces behind change in urban centres and their hinterland has safeguarded this continued invulnerability. Peasant communities maintained a mode of production which was founded on subsistence. Subsistence ensured that the peasantry lived within a basically self-

Each individual peasant family is almost self-sufficient; it itself directly produces the major part of its consumption and thus acquires its means of life more through exchange with nature than in intercourse with society. A smallholding, a peasant and his family; alongside them another smallholding, another peasant and another family. A few score of these make up a village …

Karl Marx: *18th Brumaire of Louis Bonaparte*

contained and self-maintaining system. In Ireland peasant society could endure as long as families were able to grow potatoes, keep a cow, bake bread, and cut turf. It required a bare minimum of commerce with outside economies.

Within these communities each individual farm maintained its own independence and self-reliance. Dependent above all else on the maintenance of his land, a peasant farmer placed his family, its integrity and independence, at the apex of his values. The ability of a peasant farmer to thrive without dependence on others corresponds to the invulnerability of each peasant community to the distant centres of change.

Emphasis on kinship indicates intense preoccupation with the family. That Irish country people have attached extreme importance to who does and who does not lie within the perimeters of kin is well known. On Tory Island the reckoning of kin has created an elaborate naming system, with each section of the family giving a name to the children.* Each child on Tory receives a succession of Christian names which between them denote the complex of his relatives through as many as three generations. In much of rural Ireland the word 'friend' is used to mean a relative, while to talk of 'far-out friend' is to talk of all who are not relatives. The emphasis on kin is also reflected in economic practices. Where seine- and drift-netting along the west coast required numbers of men in co-operation, the fishing was usually based on 'family boats'. In northwest Donegal, where the salmon run passes close to the headlands and islands, the fishermen have been drift-netting for six or seven weeks each summer over many decades. Today, many families have moved from islands to the mainland and some of the family crews have ceased to live in the same communities. But they remain family boats, despite the trouble of getting the crews

---

* See J. R. Fox, 'Structure of personal names on Tory Island', *Man*, 192, 1963, pp. 153–5.

Then I turned my eyes towards the slip and what did I see but one of the big black beetles walking out towards me. My heart leapt. I caught hold of my aunt's shawl, crying, 'Oh the beetle!'
'Have no fear,' said she, 'that is a curragh they are carrying down on their backs.'

Maurice O'Sullivan: *Twenty Years A-Growing*

together from mainland and island each evening.* Similarly, crews of seine-netters in the southwest of Ireland – each one needing a dozen men or more – were family teams.

Use of extended family teams involving cousins and beyond was however an exception. Almost all economic activity was carried out by the nuclear family of each household: grand-parents, parents and children, with perhaps an unmarried brother or sister of the father. Each such household saw to its own subsistence. It is no coincidence that the traditional fishing boat of the west of Ireland is the *curragh*: a boat made by stretching tarred canvas over a wooden frame, light enough for one man to carry, and just large enough to hold two or three people.† Preoccupation with the range of kin has its centre in the house-hold. Each household depended on the land belonging to one farmer. Emphasis on independence, therefore, concerned the basic farm-family unit, and not the carefully accounted kin. Mutual aid was between households, not between families.

The independence of community and household obviously could not be absolute. Inevitably even the remotest Irish com-munities came to have some involvement with markets. And

* For details of this change and its historical setting see F. H. Aalen and Hugh Brody, *Gola: The Life and Last Days of an Island Community*, Mercier: Cork, 1969, pp. 86 ff.

† The many types of *curragh* used in Ireland as well as the fishing tackle which went with them are described by E. Estyn Evans, *Irish Folk Ways*, London, 1961, pp. 233–52.

each change after the great famine meant more use of markets and more outside supplements to subsistence, while inside the communities households developed an intricate pattern of independence. In theory, since land and labour – the only two means of production – were provided by the family itself, there was no dependence on any who lay outside the household. In reality, however, this invulnerable self-sufficiency did not exist. No household could be truly invulnerable: sickness, shortage, old age – many misfortunes could happen. At any moment it could have been necessary or immensely useful to call upon the help of others. But in order to guarantee that others would be *willing* to help, it was necessary to have established a claim. Such claims, built up by giving help, were investments for the future.

This form of mutual aid compounded of claims and counter-claims between farm households, has prevailed in virtually every society where small farming has been the basic activity.* In a West Country village in England 'kinship and neighbourliness between farmers are important as a basis for economic co-opera-tion, and considerably reduce the burden on the individual families'.† And of a village in North Wales it has been said that 'to farm in the district, a man must either have the constant, daily co-operation of his fellows, or he must have a very large sum of money behind him'.‡ The Irish form of mutual aid of this kind is referred to as *'cooring'*. *Cooring* is in fact a nineteenth-century anglicization of the Irish word *'cómhar'*, which means

---

* It is interesting that Kropotkin, whose social and economic vision evolved while he lived in remote Siberian communities, saw mutual aid as the *essence* of human organization: 'The mutual-aid tendency in man has so remote an origin, and is so deeply interwoven with all the past evolution of the human race, that it has been maintained by man-kind up to the present time, notwithstanding all vicissitudes of history' (*Mutual Aid*, Penguin Books, 1939, p. 180).

† W. M. Williams, *A West Country Village*, London, 1963, p. 49.

‡ Isabel Emmett, *A North Wales Village*, Routledge & Kegan Paul, 1964.

co-operation in agricultural work and was especially used to refer to exchanges of labour. Neighbours once established in a *cooring* relationship looked to one another for help when their own household could not provide sufficient labour for a task: when the harvest work was too onerous or hurried, when the turf had to be hauled in a few fierce days, when the household was just too small.

There is little evidence that precise calculation of debt and credit in the *cooring* existed in Ireland. It seems that details were vague, and the fact of the relationship more important than the memory for particular exchanges that occurred in it. What a household knew was the neighbours they could look to for help, and to whom they would not refuse to give help if asked themselves. Conrad Arensberg in his book *The Irish Countryman* noted the intensity with which these obligations were felt, and remarked that 'failure to fulfil the pattern of conduct demanded by the obligations of "friendliness" may bring punitive action on the part of aggrieved kindred' (p. 68).

Cooring, like all mutual-aid systems, can be understood as a pre-industrial or pre-money banking scheme. In the famous trade feasts among northwest coast American Indians, surplus and riches were given away with seeming abandon. But the giving established debt and status, as well as insuring the circulation of goods and money. These guaranteed returns: the giver, by giving, guaranteed that he would be the receiver in the future. In that way the giving of surplus to friends and neighbours is not very far from the giving of surplus to a cashier in a bank.* The quality of integrated society, like the legal rules of banking, guaranteed that the gift would not be forgotten and a future claim ignored. In the case of rural Ireland, it was not surplus of foodstuff which was 'banked', for both surplus and

* See Andrew Vayda's exploration of this theme in 'Pomo Trade Feasts', G. Dalton (ed.), *Tribal and Peasant Economies*, New York, 1967, pp. 494–501.

shortage were likely to be shared by all households: in a good year all households had plenty of potatoes, in a bad year all had too few. But in *cooring*, labour played a much more significant part than produce. A household offered surplus labour to a neighbour, and so 'banked' labour for the future, establishing that in a time of difficulty they would be able to draw on others for help.

In its every detail *cooring* gave emphasis to the primacy of the basic household unit. It constituted, of course, a large qualification to the independence of the household. At a more important level, it demonstrated how each farm determined to maintain *itself*. For *cooring* protected the farm family, giving it an ability to endure in times of misfortune just as it made harvesting, thatching, and work at the bog all that much more efficient. Basic to this mutual aid is a definition of the household as the most important unit in the society as a whole. Quite simply, mutual aid is always designed to aid something: among Pomo Indians of northern California it was the tribe as a whole which benefited from the exchange feast; among the peasants of Ireland it was the household. It was not the case in the west of Ireland that the family, as delineated by the complex reckonings of a kinship system, received protection from *cooring* relationships. The confusion of mutual aid with emphasis on the broad spectrum of kin probably arose because the width of each household's kin included a majority of likely or possible *cooring* partners. But this correspondence was a consequence of that width. In most communities in the west, two or three surnames are dominant, and people are able to reckon a very sizeable proportion of their neighbours as 'relations'. But the breadth to this consciousness of kin signifies an attention to family which receives its fullest emphasis in the household. Since the economic structure had such households as its main pillar, neither the emphasis nor the nature of *cooring* are surprising.

Yet *cooring* did involve a tension at the normative level.

Although it protected the family units against difficulties and needs arising each season or at some unknown point in the future, and gave an overall security, it still created a theoretical contradiction.

Pride in the family farm's independence blended with pride in family. The strengths of the households were valued, and strength meant self-reliance; hence self-reliance was valued. The sense of family and farm as the most important bonding unit, based on its central position in the economy, was also expressed and reinforced by the Roman Catholic view of the nuclear family as the fundamental and irreducible means to a good life outside holy orders. In every aspect of the socio-economic system, as in the culture and ideology it supported, the highest value attached to the independent farm household. But the practice of interdependence created, at least in theory, a tension: *cooring* and the value of household self-sufficiency are in opposition. This opposition is observable in a contradiction which can still occasionally be heard in the Irish countryside: a farmer proudly states how he is beholden to no one, that he manages well with the family at home; he then points out how many people owe him a good turn, how he can always look to one neighbour or another for a hand if need be. In this contradiction, the farmer strongly affirms his success on two counts: on the one hand he is proud of his independence, on the other he is proud of the interdependence to which he is party.

This opposition between the independence and integrity of family farms on the one hand and the importance of inter-dependence and *cooring* on the other, did not disrupt traditional Irish life. *Cooring* ensured a high degree of social interaction: whatever its manifest functions, the latent functions – parties, meetings, communality of every kind – help make a vital and integrated society.* However much a household valued its own

*Many writers have pointed to this feature or latent function of mutual aid. See for example J. V. Freitas Marcondes: 'The day almost

One of the most pleasing characteristics of manners in secluded and thinly-peopled districts, is a sense of the degree in which human happiness and comfort are dependent on a contiguity of neighbourhood.

William Wordsworth: *A Guide to the English Lakes*

self-sufficiency, its vulnerability could never be eliminated by farmers living on poor soil and forever paying a large proportion of their extremely limited cash earnings to landlord and Church. And while the vulnerability persisted, participation in community life, in mutual aid and the multitude of social relationships it involved, could not be sacrificed to any idealization. The absolutely basic position of the household, its land and labour, in such uncertain conditions guaranteed life to the community. This life, intimately bound as it was to the opposition between two elements of the social form, obscured any problems to which this opposition might have led. Once the communities and families were radically disrupted, however, tension between household and community helped bring a series of drastic and damaging changes.

The small farms of the west still offer little more than subsistence. Indeed, population decline has reduced the labour available: it is probably more difficult today than ever in the past for a household to maintain the family land. Neither the capital for mechanization nor the mentality and conception it requires have helped withstand economic weaknesses arising from depopulation. The *West Cork Resource Survey*, for example, discovered in 1963 that in the county's southern and western regions the households consumed a large part of their farm

_____

always ends in a fiesta which strengthens a moral obligation between the one who sought the co-operation and those who participated' ('Mutirao or Mutual Aid', *Rural Sociology*, 13, 1948, p. 374).

produce at home. Over West Cork as a whole the *Survey* estimated that only £19 was earned for every £100 of gross output. This meant that the range of annual net earnings from these farms was from £5 to £45 a year.* These figures differ only slightly from those for fifteen- to thirty-acre farms in Northern Ireland in 1929, where the average for a forty-farm sample was an annual net deficit of £7.† Table 2 (p. 140) gives detailed information on small farms in County Cork.

Much of the farming in the west is still not based on markets or even the earning of money. But the households depend *more* on money than ever in the past. It is of course remittances from abroad and supplementary income from relief and local employment which remove this apparent paradox. Despite those sources of income, however, most households continue to farm on a significantly reduced scale.

The combination of changes which have occurred in the west of Ireland would all seem to heighten the importance of *cooring*. Decline in population, the isolation of so many farmers, a shortage of young people in the homes, the consciousness that vulnerability is greater for almost all houses, the altogether uncertain future – all these would seem to give mutual aid a much greater role in the livelihood of those farmers who remain in the countryside. Yet *cooring* has all but disappeared from the life of the rural people. Despite their increased exposure to shortage and isolation, Irish farmers do not seem to find any use for intricate bonds of debt and credit; they appear to have abandoned the 'banking' of surplus labour. In a situation of ever greater vulnerability the one established defence of households is apparently being ignored.

In fact, remittances from children abroad have undermined the manifest functions of mutual aid. Farm families are today

* *West Cork Resource Survey*, Dublin, 1963, c32–c48.
† For these and many more details of agriculture in Northern Ireland see J. M. Mogey, *Rural Life in Northern Ireland*, London, 1950.

Table 2: Breakdown of farm economy in West Cork for farms of 30 acres and less

A. Composition of farm output (£)

	family farm income	total output	cattle, sheep and pigs	poultry and eggs	dairy products	grain and root crops	misc.	farm produce used in home	farm management and investment income
average per farm	174·6	305·7	127·8	7·4	102·9	15·8	5·8	45·9	−154·3
average per acre	10·6	18·6	7·7	0·5	6·3	1·0	0·3	2·8	−9·4

B. Livestock numbers on farms

	Cattle			sheep		pigs			poultry	horses	total livestock units
	cows and heifers	over 2 years	under 2 years	over 1 year	under 1 year	sows and boars	stores over 14 wks	8–14 weeks			
average per farm	5·1	0·3	4·8	2·0	2·7	0·2	0·7	0·6	15·1	0·9	9·7

C. Cropping pattern on farms (acres)

	wheat	oats	barley	potatoes	sugar beet	feed roots	kale	pasture	hay	other
average per farm	0	0·9	0·4	0·5	0	0·4	0·1	8·6	3·1	0

Source: West Cork Resource Survey, Dublin, 1963.

short of money, and the emigrants' and migrants' earnings go to provide against that shortage; money is an alternative to subsistence, the remittance buttresses it with cash. In that way, remittances and *cooring* can be seen as functional alternatives.

But what the remittance does not do is supplement shortage of labour. In a few cases, sons perform both services by bringing home money and then staying for that period of the year when a dearth of hands on the farm is most critical. But they are exceptions. In the great majority of instances, shortage of labour is reflected in contraction of agricultural activity. A household, that is to say, cultivates what it can, looking to neither *cooring* nor migrants for help. The emigrant's remittance therefore represents a functional alternative within a changed situation. When farmers wanted to maintain the productivity of their lands, the remittance was inadequate. Now that farming itself has ceased to be compelling, shortage of labour is less likely to induce anxiety.

The other function of *cooring*, however, was security for the future. The existence of mutual-aid relationships constituted a good insurance against possible future difficulties. Remittances fulfil that condition also. With money to spend in village shops, householders will be able to provide for themselves – whatever happens. If necessary they can abandon the subsistence element altogether and live as if they had incomes. There are elderly people who have come to depend more on money from abroad than any source of income close at hand. And perhaps a majority of more isolated country people can anticipate the advantage of that change as they get older. Also, the vulnerability of the traditional farm has in considerable measure ceased to exist. Contraction of the farm has meant that one or two men can always maintain it. If they fall ill, then there are sickness benefits, and a neighbour who would milk the cows. But that is the last vestige of mutual aid: often enough the neighbour will be paid for his work.* On a minimized farm the future does not threaten farming, while supplementary incomes give insurance against the equally minimized misfortunes that could strike.

The traditional social system, as discovered in family and farming, forced any real surplus of labour off the land and effectively out of the country. These emigrants have become a basis of support formerly secured by a complex system of mutual aid. Of course, emigration has been a feature of country life as long as the tradition which created it, but the displacement of the key functions of mutual aid arose only with revision of attitudes towards farming. Over the many decades when high levels of emigration were taking the additional men and women out of the countryside, an alternative to *cooring* was being prepared. In the last decades, in the period since the 1930s, that alternative has come into its fullest use.

Once the manifest function of mutual aid was undermined, and the system began to be replaced by a quite different economic form, its latent functions were also displaced. Remittances from abroad do not create *ceilidhes* or celebrations. Indeed, they give no rationale for visiting and talking away the evenings. The

---

The last stronghold of national peculiarity can be found in its traditional diversions, and without diversion and amusement a culture and a race cannot survive.

Malinowski: *Argonauts of the Western Pacific*

---

*I know of two men in north Donegal who pay each other £1 a day for helping with cutting turf. First one pays for work on his turf, then the next week the second pays the first for work on the second's turf. Inevitably they end up paying one another almost identical sums: they always work in partnership and cut equal amounts. When I remarked on this to one of them he said that were it not for the money neither would be sure of the other's continuing help.

new sources of support are in fact quite opposite in quality to *cooring*: money is transferred privately, and dependence is on the closest kin. The immediate household family now does in private what neighbours used to do in public. Remittances are sent by sons and daughters, and no detail of their source and value need be known to the community as a whole should a household prefer to keep silent. And households do prefer to keep silent. The traditional emphasis on self-sufficiency of the farm family is now predominant. The replacement of *cooring* by monetary support, the shift from dependence on neighbours and extended kin to dependence on nuclear family, is completely at ease with each household's sense of itself. Values traditionally associated with the household consolidate the latest developments at the ideological level. While *cooring* corresponded to the household's need to preserve itself, it also compromised the ideals of independence. The present alternative, as well as being consistent with the most recent attitudes to farming and land, also obviates that tension between theory and practice.

Yet decline in community activity, which in part derives from and in part parallels the displacement of *cooring* and all the sociability of mutual aid, has left each household in extraordinary isolation. In peasant societies there is scarcely any part of the social structure not bound up with the particular needs and difficulties of maintaining a small farm. Absent, that is to say, are those institutions and practices which consolidate a society's community life independent of household economy. This is strikingly in contrast with the collective social activities

---

In fact, a congeries *of small farmers not co-operatively associated with one another for production, processing, buying, or selling, would be a kind of agricultural slum and in no sense a rural community.*

J. J. Johnston: *Irish Agriculture in Transition*

---

which evolve in communities left uncompromisingly committed to self-reliant households. But in Ireland, as in much of Europe and Latin America, the absence of developed institutions is a counterpart to colonialism. Religions, law-making and law-enforcement, property ownership and distribution, and 'higher' culture, have all been imposed and organized by colonials and their local agents. Consequently, household and family have increased importance and definition as the province of the farmer. As the authority and influence of householders in the community were appropriated by imperialism, their tenacity in the household increases. Alongside this tenacity goes emphasis on the household itself. And alongside the process as a whole goes a relative absence of institutionalized social life for the farmer other than the direct affairs of household and farm.* Thus when the affairs of household and farm are in decline, no broader community life can cushion or ameliorate the isolation which inevitably follows.

This privacy of the self-contained household has also received reinforcement from the intrusion of more urban conceptions of success and home. Just as farm wives often expect that a tourist is sure to prefer good white bread to the homemade 'cake', and every spot of dirt is swept from the house in the belief that an unclean home is a sign of 'backwardness', so privacy itself has come to be associated with sophistication. The home which is forever busy with the neighbours' comings and goings is seen as 'poor' and 'old-fashioned'. This conception matches social practice: households with visitors are not 'modern', at least in

---

*Imperialism also *created* alien institutions which had but meagre roots in local community life. Inevitably these impositions limited adjustment to social developments and made being Irish, Catholic and a peasant into a single identity. In the aftermath of colonization, therefore, change tends to be sudden and drastic, but social and personal readiness for such an impact is by the same token minimal. In this situation, demoralization is not easily countered.

the sense that they are more deeply implicated in traditional practices. While the most private houses – the ones which *ex hypothesi* are most willing to depend on remittances and most ready to accept contraction in farming activities – are the ones much more surely implicated in practices which are now displacing even the last remnants of the tradition. The ideas and values which have followed a deepening implication of rural Ireland with urban industrial culture as a whole are intensifying this process towards isolation. Households were theoretically individuated by tradition, but atrophy in the practices of mutual aid has come to eliminate the counterbalance to that theory. In this the idealizations of urban culture reinforce those of tradition. The isolation which these values enjoin today goes unchecked. The lonely farm houses stand apart from one another, as they stand apart from the tradition for which they were built, by both theory and practice, in a depopulating countryside.

In the fragmented society which is now becoming ascendant in the Irish countryside, co-operation between households still occurs wherever the downward trends in agricultural and social

---

'*A farm has to be big enough so that you have everything on it. It's no use if you're always to be beholden to your neighbour. It's no use if he has a horse and you haven't and you have to run to him for a loan of it. If your neighbour starts ploughing then it's time you were ploughing too.*'

quoted by James Littlejohn:
Westrigg: The Sociology of a Cheviot Parish

'*There's one thing about Ashworthy. If us be ill, or the tractor breaks down or anything goes wrong, the neighbours are always there to help.*'

quoted by W. M. Williams: *A West Country Village*

---

activity are resisted. The forms of this renewed co-operation are quite different from traditional *cooring*. They require a broad social agreement with an eye to the future of communities as a whole as well as the self-interest of each farm family. Such social agreement, however, runs counter to the mentality and pre-occupations which are dominating the country people of today.

The Road

At the northwest corner of Inishkillane parish, eleven farmers share the use of a small lane. This lane gives the farms access to the main road, and continues from the cluster of houses to the shore. Where the road reaches the shore it leads onto a stone jetty built by the Congested Districts Board at the end of the nineteenth century. At this jetty and along the beach beside there are a few *curraghs*. Three of the farmers run a line of lobster pots in the summer, and two take summer visitors for mackerel fishing in the bay or on excursions to small offshore islands. The lane had deteriorated, the surface having become so badly potted that any wet weather resulted in large muddy pools and an extremely treacherous surface. Technically the largest section of the lane was privately owned by the eleven farmers, since most of it passed through some part of the land of each. The cost of any repair to the lane, therefore, had to be defrayed among all of them. No repairs had been undertaken for decades.

The Inishkillane parish priest discovered that the county council would repair the lane if all its owners signed an agreement to that effect. The priest duly informed each owner in turn, pointing out the benefits to all of them: they would have better access to their farms; there was a strong likelihood of work on the road being offered to them; the *curraghs* at the shore would be much more easily reached by both tourist and fisherman; lorries collecting lobsters would be able to drive right to the jetty, and that would save the trouble of carrying a catch to the main road. The farmers agreed with the priest that they should sign the document, and that it would be a very good thing for all of them. The priest informed the council that the signatures would be forthcoming. It seemed that the road was going to be resurfaced.

Another reason for securing these improvements lay in the fear which a holiday house had created. An English family had succeeded in buying two deserted farms at the very edge of the jetty and were engaged in modernization. Many local people believed that these developers had bought the access from the end of the lane to the jetty. Certainly, ominous fences were beginning to appear here and there along the headland as the work proceeded. The priest, seeking to ease the apprehensions of the people, pointed out that if the county council repaired the road, it would then take over responsibility for its maintenance in future, and would by the same token ensure that no part of its access was fenced off. As the building and fencing had been proceeding, many local farmers had begun to express considerable hostility towards the English family. And at the time of these first signs of a new house and local resentments a holiday home in another part of the west of Ireland mysteriously burned down. That burning touched a memory in the people who discussed the English family in Inishkillane.

It was remembered that in the 1920s a house very close to the jetty had been burned down in protest against an English couple who had bought it and moved there in retirement. In that burning, many people claimed, the old Englishwoman had been badly hurt. Some say that she died, others that she was crippled; certainly all agree that her house was completely destroyed. The priest at that time was enraged against those in his parish who had played a part in the burning, the recollection runs. Some of the older people claim that so great was his rage that he put a curse on the community – he swore that the mackerel fishery would wither away. This curse is used to explain the present dearth of fishermen in the area. But it also gave a great intensity to discussion of the builders of the new holiday home. The priest felt sure that improvements to the lane would be secured by the considerable fear for access to the jetty aroused by the newcomers' fencing.

When the inspector from the county council came round with the documents asking for signatures, six of the farmers refused to agree. They explained that they must be *sure* they would get work on the new land before signing, otherwise they might be just giving benefit to others. The inspector had no authority to give any formal guarantee of that kind. All he could do was point out that the work would require at least eleven men, and that chances were obviously good for all of the farmers involved. Still the six men would not agree: there was no certainty, and the danger of benefit going to others was still present. The priest pointed out that the benefits were more than just the work: there was, after all, the road itself. But this did not sway them.

The road has not been repaired. The priest insists that the real reason for refusal lay in apprehension among the dissidents that the road would not be the same use to them as to others. But there are many other possible considerations: some men in the community sided with the English people building the new house, saying that they should close off access to the jetty if they wished since no one bothered with fishing very much. It is quite possible that the enthusiasm of some sufficed as deterrent to others: after all, enthusiasm must mean an eye on some real benefit, and that benefit could mean relative disadvantage. Also, thought for the future is no longer concentrated on local activities. In any case, each household, defensive of its own particular situation, was reluctant to agree with others about the overall advantage of the lane to all. They all preferred to accept its poor condition rather than run the risks they felt must come from too much co-operating.

The Pig Scheme

When the parish priest first came to Doonbere in County Cork, he decided that if at all possible average gross earnings of each family should be raised to £1,500. Influenced by the *West Cork Resource Survey*'s findings, he came to the conclusion that the one way in which this could be done was by pig breeding.

Pigs have a number of advantages to the small farmer. A valuable stock does not use a valuable pasture; with the use of prepared feed they are not a great deal of work; they are capital- and not labour-intensive; they can be sold as piglets for fattening and need not therefore be vulnerable to the many virulent pig diseases. After consultation with national and local agricultural authorities, it was agreed that a pig fattening station would be built by the government in the market town nearest to Doonbere and a large number of similar surrounding parishes. Capital required for the building and running of the station was volunteered by the government. Prices for piglets would be guaranteed, and buying would be organized on the model of the National Creamery. All Irish farmers are familiar with the Creamery and have over many years had some profit from it.

Provided with such a constant market for piglets and with guaranteed prices, it was estimated that a farmer could make about £100 per sow per year – allowing for two litters, ordinary losses, prepared feed, and the minimum regular prices. Thus

---

This is an enterprise for which acreage of land is not a limiting factor, and consequently is particularly suitable for the small-holdings in the area. There would seem to be good economic opportunities for the production of bonhors* *in this area and the enterprise would be more profitable on some of the farms than fattening purchased pigs.*

[* piglets]   *West Cork Resource Survey*

---

ten sows would each year earn £1,000. Money earned from the scheme would then be used for small but crucial improvements to the cattle and cows on each farm – better stock for example – which would push gross annual takings to the desired £1,500 per annum.

The government would build the station when the farmers combined to guarantee a supply level to give a constant stock of five thousand fattening pigs. The priest and officials involved had to urge a measure of agreement upon the farmers as a whole. To do this a host of meetings were called in local villages, at which officials from the Department of Agriculture explained all the scheme's workings and advantages. Once this was done, the farmers were asked to give their criticisms and finally their verdict. The verdict had to be collective, since the guarantee had to be for a total supply.

After several months of discussion and thought the farmers rejected the scheme. It is difficult to unravel the reasons which motivated this rejection. The priest told me, and many of the farmers said the same when discussing it, that the womenfolk did not like pigs. One man summed it up on behalf of them all: 'We'd drive the women away over the hills.' The women certainly do not like keeping pigs, because as things are it is they who must boil the potatoes which make up the main part of the pigs' feed. But under the scheme the feed would not be potatoes and that part of the work would be removed. The farmers were well aware of this, but still insisted that pigs were nasty, dirty, generally undesirable beasts. That they should use the stigma so often associated with pigs is strange: many of them have a pig or two, and all of them have had pigs from time to time in the past and are likely to have a good few more; also, two of the most respected farmers in the parish have pigs and intend to expand their piggeries. Finally, County Cork has more pigs than any other county in Ireland: prosperous pig farming in East Cork is renowned throughout the country.

One farmer who is at present planning his own piggery told me that he thought pigs were a good business proposition, but the scheme was still no good. He explained this by pointing to the others: they would not do the job properly, but would still be getting the benefit. That man's feeling is revealing: he was troubled by the co-operative element and feared both that his work would be to the benefit of his neighbours and that he would be led into dependence upon other households. Either he was to do it himself or he would not do it at all.

Generally, when talking to me of the scheme, the farmers were scornful of seeking such benefits from farming at all. Any scheme of that kind quite obviously requires a great deal of effort and that effort in turn depends on some willingness to make improvements. Moreover, the scheme entailed a relationship between farmers which has never had any place in the country life and is at odds with forces which are coming to dominate the situation at present. Schemes of this kind aiming at agricultural development and based on agreement between farmers are unlikely to succeed simply because farming is in the process of being devalued, while the individuation of each household has never been so extreme.

The social and economic separation between households, with its new emphasis on privacy, has created a great deal of suspicion. Neighbours suspect one another of receiving far more income from their family abroad than is admitted. Eyes are keened for the signs: a new dress, repairs to the house, a journey to visit relatives in the city.... Interest in the neighbours may

---

When the community is decaying social opinion degenerates into gossip, that is, instead of being interested in matters of public character, it becomes absorbed in details of private life.

W. I. Thomas and F. Znaniecki:
The Polish Peasant in Europe and America

be no more today than in the past, but the remittance to each household does not have the conspicuousness of farming or *cooring*. And the remittance has become an integral part of rural life.

Consciousness of neighbours' activities is as great as preoccupation with their earnings. Again, the reduced scale of community activities and the neighbourliness in which they were expressed has made activity less public. This privatization of life intensifies the disposition to watch others: methods if not motives must be more developed. In a Connemara village I experienced the methods in their richest and most imaginative form. At night the louder noises made outside the house by the family directly neighbouring the farm where I stayed could be heard distinctly: a visitor's arrival could be noted, as also the banging of a car door and noise of an engine starting up. Sitting around the fire in the evenings these occasional noises penetrated our conversations. As soon as a first noise was heard from the neighbour's, one of the family would jump up, open the door, and stand there listening and looking for more clues. All other preoccupations immediately gave way to overwhelming interest in noises around. When there no longer seemed to be any likelihood of any more clues being carried on the night breezes, speculation began in earnest. Everyone in the house constructed from a few and often quite uncertain sounds the entire situation surrounding them.

From a small car's arriving, staying half an hour, then departing, it was decided that John-Jo had come the fifteen miles from Oughterard to pick up the neighbour's son Paddy; no, they wouldn't be taking Katie along – the old grandmother, the mean old woman, would want her at home and not going off to the dance; no, John-Jo wouldn't be staying for tea – he could never get along too well with Katie's sister who was at home for a week or two's holiday – sure, they're never too easy with the girls who go off to that hotel work in Galway; they'll be making

off to the bar in Maam, the two young devils – but they're a
great couple of lads thank God; but they could be discussing
the journey to London – you can see going away in the eyes of
the two of them. That was Mrs Joyce shouting after them;
telling them to keep out of the bars and to stay in some other
house if there's too much drink taken; she had a troubled look
about her this afternoon, thinking of John-Jo and Paddy away
out at night in town as likely as not....

Awareness of neighbours in all its insightful detail has a
partner in gossip. The implications of all the data which are
culled from watchfulness and deduction are analysed and elabor-
ated in great proliferation. Gossiping for the most part takes
place in the village shop. Gossip is directed, of course, against
deviation. To this end it watches, anticipates and criticizes. It
is the expression of a collective Sherlock Holmes, as it were,
seeking to find in the smallest detail a clue to the identity of
transgressors and the precise nature or timing of transgressions.
A very important feature of gossip in the traditional integrated
community, therefore, is the considerable measure of agreement
about what counts as transgression: its impetus comes from the
struggle against deviation and illegality, and its methods are
collective. Without agreement it would be confused and without
any clear purpose or direction. Without agreement, gossip
becomes conspiracy.* Also, without any coherent identification
of the illegal, no gossiper can be sure of another; as well as
being chaotic, gossip becomes more difficult.

This kind of muddle and difficulty *has* disturbed the pattern

*cf. 'The members' activities are known to all; none can escape
the sanctions of gossip and public opinion. In these conditions, people
tend to reach consensus on norms and exert a consistent informal
pressure on each other to conform. This is the way a tradition is per-
petrated, relatively immune from change as long as the network
remains intact' (Josephine Klein, *Samples of English Culture*, Routledge
& Kegan Paul, 1964, vol. 1, p. 128).

An' for yer lives don't wan of ye breathe a word about what ye had in the mornin' if they ask ye at school.

Peadar O'Donnell: *Islanders*

of gossip in the small communities of rural Ireland. Traditional conceptions and collectivity itself have both been either qualified or displaced. This gives uncertainty to gossip, and the uncertainty is revealed in the great concern for secrecy. The routine 'between you and me' of all gossip has assumed a new and inflated importance. The two main consequences of this are: a circle of confident gossipers narrows to a trusted few, and comprises scarcely any beyond the household; matters gossiped about, including as they do any signs of urban success in the private home, exclude almost nothing. These tendencies are further aggravated by suspicion and competitiveness in a changing situation.

Consciousness of neighbour and gossiping both mirror in the household and its daily life the changes which have been occurring in the quality of community and co-operation. But it is in relation to more personal aspects of life that the younger people can define their relationship to community and farm life as a whole. This will be returned to in the next chapter, but the huge gulf opened up between young and old by these preoccupations with concealed features of their neighbours' lives should be noted here. The young more certainly identify themselves with modern competitive people. They also are much better able to discover what is most secret: the money other young people are injecting into the families. Similarly, the young are more closely in touch with that part of the population which expresses most change – their own friends who are thinking of leaving. Thus the young are most implicated in the one tension which still makes an uneasy bond between households.

The men who remain in the community, assuming responsibility for household and farmlands, must accept the separation and all the confusion it entails. In accepting a duty to the land, these men, despite all the changes and transformations the west of Ireland has undergone, are part of the long tradition of peasant life. To desert the family farm in favour of some more profitable and attractive location is to break with the most enduring part of Irish rural life.* Equally, to be attached to a particular farm is to be alienated from the conception of economic self-advancement that is endemic to industrial capitalism. To subordinate profitability to location as the small peasant farmer does, and to deny the primacy of material advance over all things, is at odds with the individualistic urban culture of which the Irish people are becoming a part. The farm household is committed to the farm, and is not free to pursue whatever economic opportunity may present itself.†

The extremely private household of today, moreover, has tended to scale down its farming. The degree of subsistence has declined, and in its place is the cash purchase, made possible by remittances and other concealed cash earning. Small farm households have money to spend, and many appetites and needs to cater for. It follows that there are markets available, and they are markets which have a longer term than those which were allegedly created by starvation during the great famine. Into

* K. H. Connell quotes the adage: 'Let any man go down to hell and open an Irishman's heart ... the first thing writ across it was land.' See his The Land Legislation and Irish Social Life, Economic History Review, 2nd series, XI, 1, 1958, p. 5.

† As early as 1909 it was remarked that 'By mutual help, and by common organization for common objects, the isolated and unprogressive peasant owner, while not sinking by strengthening his individualism, is lifted to a competitive level, from which he can conduct his industry on the most advanced lines, and with every resource that rivalry in the modern market requires' (William P. Coyne (ed.), Ireland Industrial and Agricultural, Dublin: Dept of Agriculture, p. 231).

these markets have stepped traders and shopkeepers. Small, isolated, unco-operative homes offer good prospects to the new entrepreneurs. But the farmers who live in the homes are there because of commitment to the land. Divided from one another's economic lives, the households which make up today's communities are acutely vulnerable to the newest version of the *gombeen* man. Protection against this exploitation, once possible in the form of community and co-operation, no longer exists.

There was a girl here had been to America ... came back, and one day she was ... in a curragh, *and she looked back and there behind the* curragh *was the 'Gan Geann', the headless one.... But a gold pin that was in her hair fell out, and into the sea, that she had brought from America, and then it disappeared ... and her sister said, 'It's well for you that it fell out, for what was following you would never have left you, till you threw it a ring or something made of gold.'*

recorded by Lady Gregory in:
Visions and Beliefs in the West of Ireland

Walking one evening in early summer into Inishkillane village I noticed one of the Kelly family on the lane ahead of me. It was Margaret, home from her job in the Civil Service in Dublin for two weeks with the family. She was eighteen, and had been away in the city for two years. An older brother and sister were both in London – the sister married to a publican and the brother working as a barman. Margaret talked to me about these relations in London as we walked together. We made our way quickly along the twisting lane, and after about a mile came to a middle-aged man strolling towards the village. He did not turn his head as we passed him, but with a small wave just murmured a greeting. Margaret did not return the greeting. She seemed to quicken her step for hurrying by him. I recognized the man to be Cornelius Kelly, Margaret's father.

Margaret's behaviour was perplexing. After hurrying past her father, she began tittering in what seemed a paradoxical mixture of embarrassment and ridicule. She kept her eyes fixed on the road in front of her until we had walked past another bend, when she quickly looked round as if to be sure that the man was no longer in sight. Then she began talking of the old country people, the old-fashioned ways. She asked if I found country life an awful thing, and met my denials with accounts of dances, drunken men in the streets.... The conversation returned again and again to the manifest lack of sophistication in the people. Passing her father in the lane had prompted this theme.

I remarked that her father did not look well, and Margaret told me that he was in fact very ill. I asked where he would be going for the evening. 'To the O'Dwyer's bar,' she said, 'and the doctor's after saying that the drink'll be doing him no good.' 'But Cornelius Kelly is no hard drinker and rarely seen in the bar,' I replied. Margaret explained that the drink wasn't the cause of his illness, but made it worse. She also explained that if he did not go out for a drink to the bars in the village he would stay at home. 'And he is not content, sitting at home for the long evenings, and not strong enough to keep at work all those hours on the land.' Margaret then talked of the drinking in the bar, and how she disliked it. Finally, as if to emphasize the distance between her home and her father, she said her brothers would not be seen going to the bar. 'Patrick and Nealy don't go for a drink: they took the pledge and have the good sense to keep away from the stuff.'

As we came into the village street, I asked Margaret where she was going herself. 'To Michael's,' she replied, where her brother Patrick could be found, and to buy a few things her mother needed. She would get the chance, she said, to be talking with Patrick and with friends in Michael's for most of the evening.

Michael's is the village shop, named after its owner Michael Ryan. Standing behind a row of petrol pumps, its large display

windows heaped with everything which could ever be used by
local people, it is the largest and best finished building in the
parish. It is constructed from two connected cottages and two
large extensions, and has a look of spaciousness and modernity.
Its outside is impressively clean. The paved area around is used
for parking the Ryan's bright saloon car, Dormobile van and
small truck. Next door to Michael's is O'Dwyer's bar. The
contrast is striking: O'Dwyer's looks older and less formal. The
outside double doors are heavy timber, and the catches on the
inside doors are rough iron. In front of the bar building stand
two heavy brown benches, one each side of the door. Inside, the
bar is panelled with tongue-and-groove varnished timber.
There is a picture of an old steamship on one wall and religious
icons on the others. The appearance is attractive; the bar has
been well cared for for many years; it looks and feels old and
weathered. Michael's has been enlarged with breeze-blocks and
smooth white plaster, and is brightly lit. The changes have come
to dominate its atmosphere as much as its look. O'Dwyer's has
been kept in good repair, and with a coat of varnish, yearly
whitewashing, a few nails and a new panel here and there, it has
been well protected against any sense of collapse or decline in
the building itself. But the changes have protected the place;
confined to 'patching-up', they could never have come to
dominate or reverse its mode. Both bar and shop make a good
living: the difference does not reflect economic disparities so
much as the use to which earnings are put. Michael's is turned
into bright modernity; O'Dwyer's keeps alive its established
style.

Cornelius Kelly walks to O'Dwyer's, and Margaret overtakes
him on her way to Michael's. At the bar, Cornelius meets other
farmers. All the bars – O'Dwyer's is the largest and most popular
of five – are regularly visited almost exclusively by householders.
But the householders who most need to meet others and who find
the greatest pleasure in the bars are the bachelors. In Inishkillane

almost exactly one half of the farms are inhabited by bachelors. Their relatively greater need for the bar as well as their large numbers gives them a striking dominance in bar life.

Now that the households are highly individuated, the bar is a focus of community life. It is the place where men can meet and discuss. It is especially significant, therefore, that a preponderance of the men who meet in this focus or centre of community are unmarried. Just as bachelors occupy so many of the farms, so they have also moved to the centre of their society. Moreover, as suggested in Chapter 4, the bachelors are men who have become reconciled to a duty to the land, who have come to accept the inevitable reduction of farm activity, who in many cases depend on remittances from their brothers and sisters abroad instead of on land and neighbours. Bachelors directly experience the worst by-products of population decline, and for most of the year evidence their acute demoralization by withdrawal and despondency. It is those people who have suffered most directly from social and economic atrophy who play the largest part in the bar.

Domination of the bar by householders, unmarried or married, means that it is the province of men who are most committed to remaining on the land. The majority of regular

---

It sounded as if the men were strangling or murdering each other, and it seemed almost miraculous that they should be able to manage their canoe. The people seemed to think they were in no special danger, and we went in again to the fire and talked about porter and whisky (I have never heard the men here talk for half an hour of anything without some allusion to drink), discussing how much a man could drink with comfort in a day, whether it is better to drink when a man is thirsty ... and what food gives the best liking for porter.

J. M. Synge: *In Wicklow and West Kerry*

---

drinkers are men who cannot leave without taking wife and children with them or finally abandoning the family farm to emptiness, sale, or the Land Commission. The society of the bar, therefore, is a society of people who have, for better or for worse, chosen a future on the land. In summer this society is vitalized by tourists, but the vitalization derives from the need for reassurance this group so profoundly feels precisely because they have a farming life. To enter O'Dwyer's, for tourist and local alike, is to enter into the society of farming men. At the centre of this society are bachelors and family men; at its outer perimeter are the women. This graduation can be represented by a diagram:

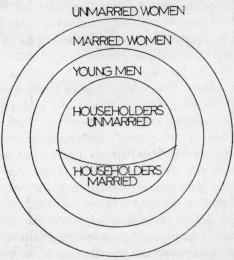

UNMARRIED WOMEN

MARRIED WOMEN

YOUNG MEN

HOUSEHOLDERS
UNMARRIED

HOUSEHOLDERS
MARRIED

The people furthest from the circle's hub are least likely to go to bars and least at ease with the bar's ways. By the same token, they feel least committed to life in the farming society.

Michael's, acting as focus as well as shop, has a quite differently composed 'society'. Women meet in the shop: for them it is the place outside home where they can go whenever they like without offending against the deeply felt privacy which surrounds farm houses. There they spend many hours choosing things they need to buy, gossiping with the shopkeeper's wife and family, meeting with friends. The shop offers women exactly what the bar offers bachelors and farmers: an alternative to isolation at home. But the shop is also used in the evenings by the younger people in the community. The young who are home from city jobs for a visit meet one another there, while school-leavers gather with some of the young men who work for the county council or in the few jobs available to them in a nearby town.

Michael's stays open late into the night. Often a group of people are still talking there when the bars close. Some women make additional shopping expeditions long after dark. People who meet and talk there are continually buying soft drinks and eating ice cream or chocolate. Just as the older farmers next door gather together with glasses in hand, so the younger men and women are holding their bottles of Lucozade or Coca-Cola. On hotter nights in summer the similarity is more conspicuous: outside O'Dwyer's, on the long wooden benches and leaning against the walls of the building, groups of men stand and talk with their glasses of beer; outside Michael's stand groups of non-drinkers.

An important difference between the shop and the bar lies in the relationship they have to tourism. Tourists are naturally less likely to spend time at a village shop; they are obviously more attracted to the society of the traditional sector of the community. But the Inishkillane people who frequent the shop do not seem interested in having tourists join them. Indeed, they seem embarrassed and unwelcoming in the presence of strangers. Analogies between shop and bar societies thus derive from activities – drinking, grouping, talking late into the night. Social composition and many of the attitudes of those who frequent the two places are strikingly opposite.

The circle which represented the bar society can be redrawn for the shop society:

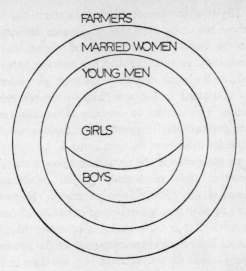

FARMERS

MARRIED WOMEN

YOUNG MEN

GIRLS

BOYS

At the hub of this second circle are those people placed at the outer edge of the bar circle. Equally, at the outer edges of the shop circle are just those people who stand at the very centre of bar life. Those who spend most time and feel most at ease in the shop are those furthest removed from farm work. It follows that they are also most removed from any commitment to staying in the countryside at all.*

The shop circle's tendency to keep its distance from tourists is a corollary of its relationship to farming life itself. It was argued earlier that the most important function of the tourist for the bar community lay in the reassurance provided by his presence in the bar. In coming to the countryside the tourist can be seen to affirm *his* liking for the entire fabric of Irish

* It is significant that the younger bachelor farmers occupy the same position on both diagrams. They are integrated fully into neither of the possible community centres. A middle position on both diagrams could be said to represent a confused and ambivalent situation in the rural community as a whole.

country life. It is the householders, particularly the bachelors among them, who most need that reassurance. By analogy, the people in the shop – the young men and women who are less deeply implicated and feel that they are well able to leave when they wish, and who no doubt for the most part have a fixed intention of leaving in the near future – do not need those reassurances. The tourists do *not* come to see them, and in so far as their presence implies approval for tradition it also implies disapproval for those bent on repudiating it.

The one place outside the home which people regularly visit thus identifies their relationship to the community. The implications of this identification are many. The two groups represent a division that has its origins in traditional community and family life. But in those traditional contexts the division in role entailed neither different evaluation of the present, nor a divisiveness within the society itself. Nor was there in the traditional context any enduring division based on individual decisions. Today young men in the community express their thinking about the future and attitudes towards the land by going either to the bar or to the shop; the choice between the two involves decisions that undermine socially determined roles and status. Instead of behaving in accord with social positions or traditional roles, the younger people make crucial decisions and judgements which spring from a personalized sense of self; they feel they should make up their own minds.

There are many farmers and householders whose positions have been largely determined by forces beyond their control. The older men married at a time when traditional ways seemed to command greater respect, before so many girls had begun to repudiate a future on the farm. But all the unmarried men are now, or have been, confronted by a choice between staying and leaving. Even the last sons of a family could not have ignored the possibility of leaving – there were too many examples to follow or condemn. Those young bachelors who always go to the shop will almost certainly follow, whether last sons or not; and those who never go to the shop but drink instead in the bars, almost certainly will stay at home.

The distinction between bar or shop and the conceptions of the young men is crucial to understanding the way in which a new individualism has replaced the institutionalizing qualities of traditional life. It is almost as if another level of consciousness has become relevant – the consciousness that is more often regarded almost as the defining feature of industrial capitalism. Where in the past the roles of young country men and women were determined by sex and therewith their position in the family, which further determined the need for emigration, now the young decide their future in relation to factors which lie outside conventional institutions and aspirations. The conceptions of the young have been at least partly formed by their awareness of other possibilities. They believe in their right to act on the new conceptions and, like urban peoples, suffer considerable stress if their actions and life-styles are too radically out of harmony with those conceptions. The minds of the new generation are no longer the minds of family farmers. Their consciousness of urban forms and their individualistic pursuit of opportunity are both profoundly at odds with life on the family land. Self comes before commitment to any externally determined role, occupation or location; and where self and the demands of the past diverge, self is generally indulged. Where acceptance of the family farm is seen and felt as a sacrifice of

---

Change may be so rapid that older people who have been born in a relatively extensive world may find themselves in a contracted one.... If the younger generation, who are born to a new space–time, cannot influence the old, splitting of community consciences takes place.

Limerick Rural Survey

---

oneself to the past, it cannot endure for long. The price of sacrifice is high and once it is perceived as such, the consciousness of a people is quick to devalue the emotional currency involved. In the recent past the price for many of the men seemed to be staying alone, unmarried, on the land: duty can now be bought with remittances and an occasional visit home.*

There are of course bachelors who have not arrived at anything like a final decision between staying as a householder and emigrating. Some men are engaged in a long and strained dialogue both with their families and within themselves over the issue of staying or leaving. John Joyce, part of whose predicament I have described, is a man without any clear resolution.† There are many others, for the most part younger bachelors. By the time a man is forty, emigration is less easy and remaining at home more natural. But before they are forty these bachelors usually experience the greatest tension between demands of family or past and their own conceptions of a 'good life'. This is the only section of the community which divides its time between shop and bar, often going for part of an evening to the bar and then joining others of their peers next door for a Lucozade.

Much of what has been said already, most particularly about the atmosphere and moods of the men drinking in winter, indicates that the decision to remain at home, the conceptions which bring identification with the householders in the bar, is not without stress. Inevitably commitment to remain a bachelor on the land is neither straightforward nor emotionally in-

---

*H. Van Beinem in his study of Dublin busmen noted the same process among Irish urban people: 'We see among younger generations a process of individualization with an increasing focus on personal problems' (*Morale of the Dublin Busmen*, Tavistock Press, 1964, p. 80). In the rural communities this process has a similar quality, but in relation to the society as a whole has a quite different set of consequences and implications.

† See Chapter 4 above, pp. 123 ff.

There are, who deem that ev'ry foreign strand
  Must glitter with a golden-sprinkled sheen;
And this chimera wild obscures the beauty,
  Which haunts their native vales and mountains blue;
It makes them shun the arduous path of duty,
  And spurn the treasures where their childhood grew.

Anon: *The Emigrant* (Dublin, 1885)

vigorating. The younger people, most poignantly the women, indicate their intention to seek for themselves a better and fuller life abroad. The mythology of emigration – compounded of the exaggerations of both returning emigrants and the media which export urban capitalism as an idea in itself – informs the mood of the 'shop crowd'. The conceptions which attend the idea of urban capitalist society give greater assurance to younger people: young men and women in the shop can console one another, and can defy any creeping doubt or guilt, with the endless possibilities that are imagined to come with leaving. The men who stay have no such ready consolation. Instead, they have no fear of guilt; at least their traditional conscience is at rest.

Some men are made uneasy by the newer conceptions and feel uncertain about emigration. They are confused and often seem to be intensely disturbed. I experienced this confusion very directly when working with Jimmy Ryan. He is the youngest son of a large family. The older brothers and sisters have all emigrated. Two younger sisters are at home, still going to school. The parents are still alive, and their three remaining children live with them in an old cottage on the family land. The farm is not large, but includes some good grazing. Jimmy and his father have tried raising sheep on the rougher part of their land, and seem to enjoy the challenge of making the smallholding earn more. But the family receives most of its income from one son, who has a way of sending unusually large gifts of money from England from time to time. Either nobody knows or no one will say what the brother does in England. The family are close and the cottage stands in comparative isolation at the end of an extremely rough mountain track. Despite their income from abroad, the Ryans do not appear abnormally prosperous. Jimmy has an old car, and his mother wears a good coat. Otherwise it is a family much like most others in the neighbourhood.

Jimmy Ryan is twenty-six. He is a thick-set good-looking young man, well respected by the householders in his parish for skills as both farmer and builder, while his enterprise and his car appeal to his peers. He has renovated two deserted cottages and intends to let them for the summer months to tourists. Also he fishes for lobster during the summer. His energy and competence are prodigious. But often he is strangely tense. This tension appears to many as shyness. In the bar he is very withdrawn, often drinking for several hours without talking. Even in summer he has the withdrawn manner more characteristic of winter drinkers, and is almost completely unresponsive to tourists at all times. Unlike most of the other bachelors of about his own age who spend time in the bar, Jimmy refuses to sing. Although he drinks heavily, he never seems to become either elated or more depressed. His personality, as expressed in the bar, is strikingly rigid, his mood strikingly constant.

For part of two summers I helped Jimmy run his lobster boat. We shot and hauled three lines of fifteen pots twice each day. Only when the weather is calm is the fishing possible. Pots are set where the rocky sea-bed is shallowest, close to the cliffs and islets along the shore, and in rough weather these inshore places are wild and dangerous. In a turbulent sea a small boat could easily and quickly be swamped, and escape would be impossible. Jimmy was not afraid of unsettled weather, but rarely took real risks. Only when a storm blew up after he had shot his pots, threatening to tear all the lines out to sea, would he take his small wooden boat into danger.

Jimmy divides his time more or less equally between shop and bar. His friends tend to be in the shop – people he was at school with who have also fished for lobsters. Once he went to Dublin to work, but returned. He says that the family asked him to come home, but one of his close friends claims that Jimmy was miserable in the city. The friend also says that one of Jimmy's cousins in America is forever trying to persuade Jimmy to join him there. When he discusses the life he has at home and the advantages of going away, Jimmy becomes very inarticulate, mumbling his way through extremes of both apprehension and enthusiasm at the prospect of life in England. He predicts that he will go, but insists that it can't be this month, or next winter. There is always some job to finish at home.

One morning Jimmy rushed to see me much earlier than usual. The southwest wind was beginning to blow very hard and the sea was rising. The pots were out, and he wanted to haul them before it was too rough and all were torn out to sea. We raced to the beach, launched the boat, and headed for the line furthest along the promontory – it was obviously better sense to haul the more distant and more exposed pots first. But when we came to the marker buoy, close under a low cliff, the sea was breaking along the rocks in swirls of foam. The boat had pitched a great deal on the journey out, but once the hauling began it was no longer possible to navigate into the waves: lines are always hauled towards the stern, the boat facing as the lie of the pots determines. Jimmy decided to leave the outboard out of gear but idling. It was essential to make sure the line kept clear of the propeller: to disentangle a rope in a wild sea would have been impossible.

As we hauled, the stern was pulled by the weight of the pots almost to the crest of the waves. Each time a particularly treacherous breaker began to lift and pitch the boat, the man in the stern had to pay out rope through his hands. Again and again we narrowly missed swamping. Eventually that furthest line was hauled, the few lobsters dumped to the bottom of the boat, and the pots stacked in the bow. The first and second lines were more easily secured, and though we had both been badly frightened at least the pots were saved.

Later in the afternoon, with the wind lulled and the sea slowly beginning to settle, Jimmy went out by himself and shot two lines along the promontory, this time a little closer to the beach than we had first been in the morning. Early that evening he again came to find me, saying that the sea was looking bad, the night would be stormy, and we must haul all the pots again. I protested, arguing that the wind was only gusting and would probably settle: I felt sure there would not be a storm that night. It seemed unnecessary to hazard another trip under that steep face of the headland. The pots could be hauled soon after dawn, when the sea would have settled. Fishing is rarely good in hard weather; the most we stood to gain was the price of three or four lobsters. The risk was far too great.

Jimmy insisted that we haul the pots, and that there could be a great catch the next day if we could only shoot all those lines round the other side of the bay. He was not to be dissuaded, saying he would go by himself if necessary. Eventually I agreed to go with him.

As we pulled away from the beach once again the sun was low on the horizon and the evening light was dulled by the last rain clouds which were driving in from the west. The sea was heaving more treacherously than at any time earlier in the day. As the boat came along the rocky shores we could make out the danger signals: foam rushing and eddying back from submerged rocks, and spray billowing with the rain in air currents on the cliff faces. As my fear became irrepressible I began to shout to Jimmy over the noise of sea and outboard engine my conviction that we were crazy not to go back. But

my voice was drowned by Jimmy's determination more surely
than by the noise of the storm. I began to sense that this determination went far beyond any concern with saving pots or
selling lobsters.

Jimmy's face was set in concentration. He was preoccupied
with something far beyond the technical difficulty of hauling
pots in waves and surf. At the most critical moments of the haul
– the engine was twice swamped and cut out altogether; one of
the pots jammed in the sea-bed and the strain needed to move
it pushed us to the extremest edge of danger – Jimmy laughed
and shouted his willingness to 'swim for it'. His closeness to
drowning – neither of us could possibly have 'swum for it' –
appeared to be a pleasure to him. I felt keenly that he wanted to
die. Perhaps the tremendous risks as we rocked and swayed, the
sea racing a bare inch under one side then the other and stream-
ing past the engine as the stern dipped with the strains on the
ropes, finally supplanted the anxiety which so often seemed to be
silencing him. Whether the undertaking was either consciously
suicidal or a way of displacing anxiety, it was certainly connected
at some level with Jimmy's profound malaise.

When we finally arrived safely at the beach and had hauled
the boat out of the surf, Jimmy walked back into the village with
me. He was unusually relaxed and talkative. As we came into
the main village street I suggested we go together for a drink in
the bar. He hesitated, became immediately tense again, then
said no, he had to get home, that he would call down to the bar
later that evening. He did come for a drink, barely half an hour
before closing time, and stayed for one quick pint of Guinness.
He was his usual self: tense and silent, leaning heavily on the
bar, chain-smoking and brooding. I do not know if he had spent
any time in the shop next door before coming to take his pint.

If Jimmy Ryan had spent time in the shop that evening he
would have been with people who do not share his tense
uncertainty. As farmer and fisherman Jimmy is close to the

centre of his society; his friends in the shop are or feel themselves
to be on its periphery. Jimmy is not certain what he wants his
own place to be, and cannot imagine feeling satisfied either at the
centre or on the periphery.

The young people in the shop are glad to be able to imagine
their imminent departure. They are glad because, unlike the
bachelors who cannot decide between shop and bar, they have a
consciousness of their community which combines radical
criticism with more elaborate aspirations. They see weakness
and limitation in traditional forms of life and have a mind to
achieve 'better things'. The relationship between their criticisms
and their idea of the future is important. Indeed, they proceed
in partnership, the one enhancing the other, building between
them some part of the mentality of urban capitalism in the
country people. Those who have internalized that mentality
most fully, and are set upon realizing its implications, can be
found in the shop. They are the most relaxed people in the
community, the ones who will soon be leaving it.

In this way the bar and shop societies grow from a distinction
between two consciousnesses which are continually straining
against one another in the small communities of the west. In fact
the distinction between the groups also turns in some measure
on alcohol itself. The country women, for example, rarely drink
outside their own homes, and rarely enough in them. On
Sunday evenings during the summer a few women go to a small
back room in a bar, and cluster there to share the singing and
gaiety with the tourists. But even then they do not go into the
main bar, and will not even enter by the front door, preferring
to go to the back of the house and come in through a kitchen
entrance. When in the bar those Sunday evenings few of the
women drink anything much stronger than one or two small
glasses of sherry. They certainly never get drunk. Many of the
younger people who make up the large part of the shop crowd

At a funeral in a Connemara village, a young curate, disgusted with the drunkenness, threw down the money that had been collected, and told the people that it was the price of devilry.

Irish Nation, leading article of 1909

never drink at all. Like their mothers, the younger women do not go into the bars except perhaps for half an hour on the busiest summer Sunday night of the year. Even then they do not often drink anything alcoholic. The young men who are most committed to the shop society avoid going into the bar, and will go there if asked by a friend only with the greatest reluctance. When in the bar they often drink 'pop'.

In Inishkillane parish, as in many other parishes of the western seaboard, the priest has conducted something of a campaign against drinking. In this he directs his attention at school children, especially young boys. At the time of their confirmation, when they are thirteen or fourteen, he encourages them 'to take the pledge'. They are asked as an atonement for the sins of humanity to pledge never to take alcohol. The priest never drinks and explains this in terms of religious sacrifice, noting that there is evil enough in the world, and much which has its origin in excessive drinking of alcohol, and that never to drink intoxicating beverages is small enough sacrifice. A majority of the young teenagers seem to be persuaded by the priest's arguments, and in great seriousness 'take the pledge', undertaking never to drink. Often they advertise their commitment by wearing in their lapels a small badge, signifying that they are making and will continue to make this 'small sacrifice'.

It is quite remarkable how many young men in Inishkillane take this pledge seriously. But they do not, despite the argument and theory of the priest, conceive of it as a religious act, still less as a sacrifice in atonement for humanity's sinfulness. Rather, it is part of their identification with the forces opposing the traditional patterns of social life and social authority. No householder does *not* drink, and many of the bachelors who are soon to become householders are the most conspicuous figures in the bars. The consciousness which leads people into the shop, therefore, is reinforced by the principle involved in sustaining the pledge. Whether or not the boys of confirmation age have a consciousness of their separation from the mainstream of farming life as they take the pledge is unclear, but the role which the pledge comes to have in the minds of these young men as they grow older and closer to the choice betweeen home and emigration is clear enough. Alcohol is one issue on which the division between commitment to tradition and commitment to a newer conscious-ness can focus in everyday life.

That it is used for that purpose is shown by some of the emigrants who return for summer visits. Those who have taken the pledge are sometimes there drinking tomato juice with their old friends and former companions. But several of these men have told me that they drink in England, and talk as connoisseurs of the best 'Irish' pubs in London. They are not ashamed to drink at home, they say, but just do not want to. This is not true of all the returning emigrants, of course, but involves enough to suggest that the role of the pledge is more closely bound up with attitudes towards the various sections of the community than with any religious act of self-denial. Not drinking alcohol is a social *sign* of much the same kind as spending time in the shop.

Sobriety is making way in the Ireland of today,
Fill the bumper fair, every drop is poison,
Will you walk into my parlour, said the spider to the fly,
'Tis the prettiest little drunkery that ever you did spy,
Oh, join the abstainers and you'll be the gainers ...

James Whiteside, quoted in Brendan Behan:
Hold Your Tongue and Have Another

At the centre of every parish is the Church. Traditionally, the parish priest appears as a figure of considerable formal authority and his church as the centre of a community. Religion solemnized and to some extent regulated the family and its institutions. As well as containing the rituals for each crucial event in a man's life, its ideology matched traditional social practice as a whole. Roman Catholicism emphasizes the authority of the father and the gentleness of the mother. It dignifies the celibate and the virgin. It symbolizes motherhood as sacrifice and suffering in the greatest of causes. Its moral framework includes great reverence for the close family.* The

---

Beetles: *The earwig is always killed but the beetle never. The reason is that the earwig gave misdirections to someone inquiring for Christ but the beetle spoke up and corrected him. Beetles are lucky.*
                                        Dictionary of Irish Mythology

One woman told me last Christmas that she did not believe either in Hell or in ghosts. Hell was an invention got up by the priests to keep people good, and ghosts would not be permitted, she said, to go 'trapsin' about the earth' at their own free will; 'but there are fairies and little leprechauns, and water-horses, and fallen angels'.
                                        W. B. Yeats: *Mythologies*

---

*It is the position of the woman and the prolongation of virginity – the two most striking weaknesses in post-famine tradition – which the Church has most dignified. The two qualities are secured with the single myth of the Virgin. Mary 'was the first to consecrate her virginity to God. In this way she led to God all who instated her virginity, as David has foretold: *After her shall virgins be brought ... into the temple of the King*', and Mary also 'consented to everything ... with a steadfastness that filled even the angels with astonishment' (St Alphonsus Maria de Legion, *The Glories of Mary*, Dublin, 1963 [first published 1750], pp. 72 and 164.

religious calendar corresponds to the seasonal rounds of subsistence farming. Catholicism and a peasant heritage have in
Ireland merged into a single tradition. The Church and its
priests sanctify and celebrate traditional practice. Folklore and
Roman Catholicism in rural Ireland have coloured and sub-
stantiated one another.

The bond between Church and peasantry in Ireland has been
tightened by their joint resistance to British colonialism.
Catholicism was the religion of opposition to English hegemony.
For most of the nineteenth century Catholics were deprived of all
formal political influence. With the respect accruing to religious
leadership and the literacy of the clergy, the parish priest
inevitably held a position of great importance. The success
which Catholicism had in raising funds throughout the nineteenth century testifies to this domination over the rural parishes.
At the aftermath of the great famine the Church put its influence behind the tendency towards consolidated holdings and
encouraged the delaying of marriage. The correspondence
between Church teaching and socio-economic realities thus
survived and was actually enhanced by the disruptions of the
middle part of the last century.*

But the changes did not *derive* from Church teaching or
influence. Just as the doctrines of Roman Catholicism supported
peasant life before the famine, so they endorsed a trend which
sprang from the most basic demands in the situation following
the famine. Perhaps most important of all, the Church had least
success in assisting changes required in the western districts,
where the situation was worst and the peasantry was least able
or willing to alter the shape of their holdings. Indeed, the Church
always found difficulty in innovating or straining against the
farm practice of the parishioners. It was only on the question of

---

*For support of this see K. H. Connell's essay on the Church and
marriage in nineteenth-century Ireland in his *Irish Peasant Society*,
Oxford University Press, 1968.

The country was joyless.... It will be said that the Irish are too poor to pay for pleasure, but they are not too poor to spend fifteen millions on religion.

George Moore: *Home Sickness*

marriage that Church pronouncement coincided so precisely with social need and economic possibility, making the influence of Church and priest appear paramount. The rural community accepted the Church's metaphysic virtually to a man, attended its services with unfailing regularity, depended upon its sanctifications of their *rites de passage*, passed much of their surplus money into its hands, encouraged their daughters to be nuns and delighted in a son who gained the priesthood; but the farmers farmed as they saw fit. And in truth the communities of rural Ireland have always been widely dispersed, with a majority of the population living a long walk from church or priest. The economic practice in the countryside was therefore relatively immune to the watchful eye or concerned interest of any priest bent on change.

This distinction between the sacred and the secular, with the limitation it implies on the influence of religion and priest, has become most relevant today. For it is only in the last thirty years that real and open tension has come to exist between the wishes of rural priests and their parishioners, visible, for instance, in the story of the Doonbere pig scheme told in the last chapter. Naturally enough, parish priests are disturbed by the rapid depopulation of the countryside and by the demoralization accompanying it. Impatient and unnerved by the dispirited and contracted qualities of their parishioners' social and farming lives, many priests in the west of Ireland are railing against the situation they find all around them. Sermons are again and again preached appealing to the young to stay at home and to the old to farm with greater enterprise and determination and in fuller co-operation. A parish priest in County Mayo once complained to me about the rigid way in which his flock interpreted Christian teachings on sex. 'A few illegitimacies around this parish, and you'd be believing in the spirit of the people,' was the tone of his lament.

Virtually everyone goes to church every week, and many go more often than that. And the church, like bar and shop, is a place of community and sociability. Moreover, it is the one place where everyone comes together irrespective of aspiration, consciousness, or future. A County Clare priest once told me that all but two of his parishioners went to church every Sunday if they were possibly able. I asked him how the people thought of the two who did *not* go, and was told: 'They'll be saying the two of them must be a little wrong in the head, with the claustrophobia or something of that sort. And you know, they'll be right enough in saying it.' A farmer in that parish once asked me why I did not go to church every Sunday, and I told him I was not a Roman Catholic. He replied, sensibly enough, that details of belief had no importance, that it was 'great fun, with the singing and everything' and that I was being rather foolish to miss out so badly on the weekly service, on the great crowd, and the drink taken afterwards in the village bars.

It may seem, therefore, that around the church the communities gather in solidarity, and that this solidarity offsets and qualifies the divisiveness implicit in the distinctions between shop and bar crowds. After Sunday service, however, when the greatest part of the parish spills in one crowd from the church, divisions quickly reassert themselves. Householders go to bars, and many of the women go with daughters and sons to the shop. In the streets young men gather in tight groups, not wanting to rush with the householders into the bar. This configuration of groups lasts throughout the day of worship – groups joined together by virtue of their attitudes and the futures these attitudes foreshadow, each group quite evidently distinct from the other.

Sunday may begin with mass for all, but the community returns quickly to its different sectors. Social practice and sanctification briefly merge, but it is unsanctified social practice which maintains its ascendancy.

In the small communities of today, where isolation of each household is intensified by a much-reduced population, the liking people express for church services is not surprising. Villagers genuinely feel respect and awe for their Church. But it is the religion and not the priest's assumption of secular importance or influence which is taken with great seriousness. Of course, in the area of sexual mores religion has impinged most directly on social life. I have already mentioned priests poking at hedgerows after dark in their struggle against their young parishioners' illicit liaisons. And there can be no doubt that such assiduous attentions of the priests had their counterpart in traditional conceptions. Marriage, at least since 1850, has been a matter largely of family economics. Neither romantic nor erotic ideas were regarded as any vital part of the traditional society's life – they were the province of the corrupt, debauched, magical and strange.

Yet, as already mentioned, many older people have vivid memories of gaiety and dancing which *was* manifestly sexual. Perhaps the sense of family hardened the young people against illicit intercourse, but it did not by all accounts displace

---

It is only for themselves that they seemed to be unable or, better, unwilling to imagine a sexuality without familism. Other patterns of sexual behaviour they see and have heard of, but these are immoral and unworthy ways of doing things and acting, departures from the right and normal, sometimes disgusting, sometimes ludicrous, always mysterious.

Conrad M. Arensberg and Solon T. Kimball:
Family and Community in Ireland

---

flirtatiousness or erode from their minds the romance of love. Many of the songs and ballads and folk-tales which turn on love and sex also include the magical role of an enchantress, and it is tempting to see witchcraft in traditional Irish life as the explanation of romance. But there are ballads enough which tell of love at its most human. In the secrecy which a very populous community allowed, where it was possible to enjoy a *ceilidhe* without too much notice, and where gossip was well fed with more important matters, more happy and less inhibited flirtations seem to have flourished. Indeed, it is hard to believe that a rural society – particularly one which emphasized parties and dancing as much as traditional Ireland – confined sexuality to economistic marriage. The attention which the priesthood seems to have given to the matter makes a picture of unbending repression still less plausible.

Sexual relationships – from small flirtations to copulation – are rare indeed among today's younger parishioners. This gap in the lives of rural Ireland's young can best be understood in terms of processes that have already been detailed. In the absence of a densely concentrated population, the conditions for covert liaisons and flirtatiousness are absent. There is no longer a screen between the keen eyes of gossips and the young people's activities. In a society where the traditional ethic of family is endorsed by a Roman Catholic view of sin, the covert quality of extramarital sexual life is inevitable. Also, the young people who anticipate emigration have transferred any expectation of sexual gratification – in *or* outside marriage – from home and countryside to cities far away from home. Equally, those who have decided to stay at home do so in the full realization that the decision almost certainly entails a life of chastity.

Thus the country people accept the celibacy of rural experience. The Church's teachings endorse it, despite occasional protestations of dismay at its more disastrous consequences from priests with sympathy for bachelor farmers holding out lonely

*'Ha! Ha! when the cat's away the mice will play.' That is the
only time they have for it, said I in my own mind. 'Your soul to the
devil, Michael, we are done for.'*

Maurice O'Sullivan: *Twenty Years A-Growing*

on the land. The barrenness thus inflicted on the countryside
and its people affects the prevailing consciousness of the younger
generation. And behind this ability to split sexual experience
from life in the countryside lie generations of country people
and religious doctrine which have seen in almost all natural
sexuality a profound sinfulness. Useful as those attitudes may
have been for traditional farm life, they hardly correspond to the
aspirations and preoccupations of those among today's young
who have come to see themselves as part of the broad culture
of urban capitalism. Even where it wishes otherwise, the Church
is not able to prevail against these newer ideas and village priests
have no means of persuading or demonstrating to the local
youth that life at home can offer the significant part of what they
believe they will be able to find abroad.

At the centre of traditional Irish community life was the
farmer and householder. Every feature of the society turned
upon his authority and the demands of the farm he owned. No
break has occurred between the demands of farm and the status
of farmer. But that part of the community centred on the shop
has in many crucial respects broken with the system as a whole.
The overall fabric of traditional farm society is now located, by
consciousness at least, in opposition to the younger men and
women.

The *Limerick Rural Survey*, which includes some of the most
perceptive comments ever made on rural Ireland and the farming communities, discusses the way in which women, old and
young, are held by tradition at the edges of the society. Their

peripheral position has been made more remote by all the contraction in community life. And now that the opposition is between two consciousnesses, the distance between the centres and the edges of the community circle has been vastly widened. Difference in social role and function is being transformed into qualitative difference of mind.

At the centre of the new consciousness stands the shop. Behind shop counters are shopkeepers. The shopkeepers' mentality is the most developed version of the young people's consciousness. It reverses the traditional conception of farming, family, and society itself. And profits, like the mind behind them, advance alongside the changing society. The focus of authority is passing ineluctably from householder-farmer to shopkeeper; businessmen thrive on the passing of tradition.* The isolated farmhouse, the sense of privacy, and the enlarged role of cash spending, all enhance the shopkeeper's position, providing the social context most favourable to his enterprise, and respect for himself. The shopkeeper does not usurp the role of the church. But the church does celebrate – in the form of memorials to the greatest generosities of individuals and local families – the success of the successful. And the central position of shop and shopkeepers is at ease with the division, always present even in rural Ireland, between secular and sacred. The shop, or the mentality and family behind it, is the ascendant secular influence. Only in the bar does social life not preclude some belief in farming as it has been understood for a century. The large number of older householders in the bars signifies the limits to that quality of bar life. The young, the future generation, are not to be seen giving much sign of their belief in traditional mores and activities.

One qualification needs to be added to this picture of bar, shop and church. In many communities there are a very few

* See for example Daniel Lerner, *The Passing of Traditional Society* (Illinois, 1958), particularly Chapter 1.

farmers who *do* atypically farm in a businesslike manner. These men occupy a midway position between shopkeeper and traditional householder. They are not inclined to co-operate with other farmers, but that is because they are acutely aware of the others' dislocation from the enterprise of farming. Moreover, these few men are interested in getting more machinery, and when they do have a tractor they often make some extra money by hiring it out to their neighbours. These men very rarely go to bars either in summer or winter, nor do they spend any time in the shop. They are family men, and keep themselves very much to themselves. They buy such provisions as they need, but seem no more inclined towards the small shop society than towards the society of drinkers and singers. They do go to church, and do enjoy its community, but after church they quickly go home again.

Some of these more vigorous farmers may succeed in raising and keeping another generation on their land, and they in their turn may consolidate their economic viability either by more capital–intensive farming or with expansion of their activities towards more directly profitable trades and services. In the latter case they would also come to share the position of the shopkeepers, and would, like them, be participating in the newer centres of community and finding an economic foothold in the eclipse of the tradition. They would, so to say, move into the shop.

The man slid to the ground. 'I am of the family of Baeka More,' he said. 'I have come far looking for a servant, because those I employ either run away or get killed by the giants whose land adjoins mine. No one in the surrounding country will work for me any more and so I came to Erin to get a man brave enough or fool enough to enter my employ.'

'The Widow's Son and the Little Tailor',
from Pat Mullen (ed.): *Irish Tales*

Michael Ryan is the owner of the shop 'Michael's'. There are forty-two other householders called Ryan in Inishkillane parish. Michael is the only entrepreneur amongst them. He is a heavily built man and has a curiously deliberate manner: he moves slowly, but his slowness does not evoke the unhurried country man so much as reflection and calculation. His hands are large but soft. Although he has a look of strength, his arms are not filled by toil, and his frame does not look ready for spading and stoning the hard Clare fields.

There is to Michael Ryan a confidence expressed by an air of serious preoccupation with many activities. There is not much lightheartedness to him as he works on constructing the extension at the back of his shop, sorts ropes in the adjacent storehouse, or peers into the engine of one or other of his vehicles. He does not linger to talk with the people who pass by, and appears quite satisfied with a bare nod and a minimal greeting. He does not seek other men for advice or favour as he goes about his jobs. Michael Ryan has a self-reliance, a composure even, which distinguishes his bearing and behaviour from most other parishioners. This bearing and behaviour are not subject to seasonal change: he is no more serious in winter and no less self-contained in summer. Tourists do not induce in him any public display of jocularity. His mood, like his shop, is maintained through every season. And if one time be more profitable, the advantage creates activity rather than any very obvious change in Michael Ryan's spirit.

Michael's air of self-reliance obviously contrasts with the fluctuating moods of other householders. The self-reliance and strong regard for privacy among other householders, although fortified by the traditional value of family integrity, are borne less confidently than by Michael as he quietly and seriously moves about his business. Indeed, there is a contrast in the very activity itself: the serious, almost withdrawn concentration seems to insist that even if there were the inclination there is certainly not the time for frivolity or mere sociable talk. The householders of the west of Ireland rarely give an impression of haste, and certainly would not like to suggest even by appearances that a job to be done must preclude conversation or friendliness. In these quite simple ways, Michael Ryan is unlike the great majority of Inishkillane men. His air of assurance indicates that he is not oppressed or troubled by the despondency and ambivalences which prevail among his peers.

Michael Ryan is a local man. His surname is the sign, and his is one of the many Ryan families who have lived and farmed in Inishkillane for generations. The name itself goes back to the local Gaelic lord who fought with the help of Spain against English colonialism in the eighteenth century. Michael's family held land in Inishkillane when it was rented from English landowners in the nineteenth century, and began to purchase it after the 1923 Land Act. He is not, like many of today's small country shopkeepers, a town man who has come as a shop-keeper to a country district. Nor is he part of a long established family who have come to shopkeeping from 'better things'. Moreover, his is a Catholic family: three windows in the parish church carry Michael's name, acknowledging his help with reconstruction and repairs. It is not his origins which differentiate him from others. His behaviour is not the product of a childhood in another rural area, still less in another culture.

The Michael Ryan family is, in its domestic social qualities at least, much like other Inishkillane families. Michael married a woman fourteen years his junior. She was born in a neighbouring parish and lived there until her marriage. They have had five children – three girls and two boys. The youngest is an infant and the oldest is fourteen. As well as these children and their parents, the family also includes Michael's youngest and only unmarried brother Patrick. Michael is very much the head of the family, and the division of labour by sexual roles follows traditional patterns. The two girls who are old enough help in the shop. Michael never serves in the shop, except when he must look out some piece of heavy or specialized equipment. The eleven-year-old son helps Michael when he goes to round up cattle, but does not work in the shop either. Patrick helps with driving and farming, but nothing else. In all these respects the Michael Ryan family follows the customary family life.

The children go to the local school and the family live in the main village street, but there is one important clue to the distinct position of the shop family: they are always referred to as 'the Michaels'. The son is called Patrick Michael, the daughters Mary Michael and Ann Michael, and the wife Mrs Michael. The presence of forty-two other Ryans in the same small parish naturally necessitates some way of distinguishing each family by other than the family name. What reveals Michael Ryan's significance is the fact that all other Ryans are identified by one Christian name with the Ryan, and where that is still inadequate with two Christian names. Thus there are Cornelius Ryan, Patrick John Ryan, Joseph Ryan, etc., while their wives are Mrs Cornelius Ryan, Mrs Patrick Ryan, Mrs Joseph Ryan. Mrs Michael is unique in the privilege of having her surname dispensed with. Nobody refers to her by any other name, and if her closer friends call her by her Christian name the politer way to address her is 'Mrs Michael'. By this special naming the Michaels are picked out from all other Ryans, and identified as a family that demands special treatment.

The Michaels centre their activities on the shop. Its outward appearance – the degree to which its bright modernity differs from buildings with more traditional occupants and functions – was described in the last chapter. The shop has an enormous stock. The vast range of goods is packed onto shelves which reach from floor to ceiling, cans and cartons piled one on the other in serried lines and unstable pyramids, a profusion in uncertain order making the walls a jigsaw of consumer goods. Under the counter are boxes heaped with goods which find no space on the shelves; the counter is itself littered with trays of sweets and boxes of tomatoes, filling any spare surface between cutting, slicing, weighing, and accounting equipment; where shelves reach the floor, more goods spread out into the shop's space; outhouses behind the building are filled with overflow stock and a collection of items which are too large or too esoteric to find room in the main shop areas. These piles and heaps are arranged as well as possible into groups: one area of shelving is

---

Some of them fiddle with food four times a day. At that time we used to eat as much food in one meal as in those four put together. People lasted two days on one meal of this kind, if they needed to. A man can't go a pike's length in these days without tumbling on his backside, for they don't eat a meal at all, but a miserable bite or two.

Thomas O'Crohan: *The Islandman*

---

for tins of vegetables, soups, fruits; another for washing powder
and kitchen equipment; fresh vegetables are kept close to the
counters; cured meats near the slicing machine; Wellington
boots and other footwear are at the bottom of the shelves on the
floor; fishing tackle to the right of the till; shirts in their cello-
phane covers are high on the shelves of one side; children's toys
at another; frozen foods are in a large freezer behind the counter;
ice creams are in another by the door; soft drinks are kept in
their crates on one side of the floor, opposite the boots; in the
outhouses are ropes, timber, buoys, nails, canisters of Calor
gas; smaller items of fishing tackle are inside the shop; fresh
meat is brought to individual order from a butcher relative in a
nearby market town; bread least likely to desicate with storing
is stacked in boxes by the counter, white and sweet brown in
watertight wrappings; some soda farls are for sale quite fresh
two or three times a week; flour, sugar, currants, soda – all the
requirements for home baking – are for sale in both small bags
and huge sacks; baking mixes, jelly powders and sponge-cake
mix in boxes offer the alternatives to home produce, as do the
rows of mixed fruit and jam and narrow bottles of ketchup and
brown sauces; a few pots and pans are balanced in odd
corners.

Any and every demand is anticipated by the shop, and most
of the parishioners make most of their purchases there. It is not
the only shop in the parish, but it *is* the only general store.
Some of the bars have some few items for sale, but none carries
a stock which in its voluminous heterogeneity aims at covering
all the needs of the local people. Nor is any other supplier's
home the focus of a substantial element in the community's
social life. The largeness of the supply in Michael's signals the
unequivocally entrepreneurial mentality of the shopkeeper.
This shop is not a dense muddle of odds and ends, not a dis-
organized village store which in its profusion of goods stifles
or ignores the requirements of profitability. Rather, the wealth

Arra, man, it is the way with them now, they have shoes on them as soon as they can crawl, not to mention all the clothes they wear, for all that they are weak, and will be.

Maurice O'Sullivan: *Twenty Years A-Growing*

of supplies in Michael's reflects an insight into the multitudinous needs and the potential demand for every kind of purchase which have emerged in rural communities like Inishkillane.

Similarly, it reflects Michael's understanding of just how much of their hidden earnings families are willing to spend at the village store. And he prices his goods by the same calculation: they are not cheap, there is no uncertainty as to what each thing should cost, the charges are those of a shopkeeper who is interested in advancing his business. If Mrs Michael and her two daughters sometimes have difficulty in finding an item among the plethora of goods everywhere around, they certainly do not have much difficulty in stating prices. The shop is a business, and those who own and run it are accordingly businesslike. In this respect it is not like the shopkeeping of the small bar owners, and quite at odds with the small provisioner still occasionally to be found in remote rural places. In Michael's the selling is not accompanied by any embarrassment. Not to be found in Michael's are the politeness and kindness which epitomize the small community shops owned and managed by people with the traditional consciousness that sits uneasily with the role of trader.

Michael's does not sell alcohol of any kind. His business interests do not include a bar. The contrast between shop and bar, at least in the consciousness of the groups who frequent the one or the other, has already been described. It is a contrast which is supported by Michael Ryan's own predilections. He virtually never goes into a village bar, and is the only householder in the parish who so consistently avoids bar life. Even in the high tourist season in late summer, when almost all are in their way enjoying and celebrating the liveliest weeks, Michael does not take a drink or hear out a song in any bar, nor does Mrs Michael ever join other wives on those rare Sunday nights in the back room to gossip and overhear the joys of the drinking men. There is no simple explanation for this apparent abstinence: Michael has no moral objection to a drink or two, and he certainly does not feel at ease with the crowd of younger people at his shop.

Michael's shop is also a guesthouse, and Mrs Michael must prepare meals and pay attention to her visitors when she is not behind the counter; even if she were so inclined Mrs Michael would not have the time to join the women in the back room of the bar those busy summer nights. Michael's accommodates about fourteen visitors, and its first storey has been designed with the tourist trade in mind. For those weeks when tourists are spreading into the Irish villages of the west, the Michael family squeezes into as few bedrooms as possible, leaving a maximum of space for guests, which is well filled for the six-week tourist season. In their willingness to move out of rooms to make way for paying guests, the Michael family is doing nothing either in violation of traditional conceptions of home or at odds with their less entrepreneurial neighbours. Many country people let whatever part of their houses they can to visitors in the summer. Often a family moves from their house to the byre or cowshed which was originally the family home. In almost every small village there are the signs which indicate a home trying to make some extra money from the bed-and-breakfast trade.

Yet the Michaels' style as hosts to paying guests is as different from that of their neighbours as the buildings they own are different from a country farmhouse. The sheer number of tourists they house is remarkable. Few bed-and-breakfast houses can accommodate more than four or five people, while those moving into their byre most often rent to one tourist family at a time. The number of visitors at Michael's creates a prodigious amount of work, more than they can accomplish unaided. So they pay for help during the tourist time, which makes them again unique among local guesthouses. Also, the kitchen in the Michaels' house was not able to meet the demands of so many visitors – unlike most other families which take guests, the Michaels like to provide full board – so they have built a larger kitchen as part of an extension to their house. Thus the house has been reshaped by the demands of the tourist trade.

In that fundamental respect the Michaels' interest in the tourist trade is quite distinctive. It is more of an enterprise, with the home made into something of a hotel in its subordination to the requirements of good business.* The maximizing of

---

The peasant conceives of farming as a way of life. He is a conserver of the soil. His ideas of wealth and well-being cannot be expressed in terms of profit, capital, personal comfort, or conspicuous consumption. He draws his satisfaction rather from work done well, from the improvement and increase of his holdings and herds, and from the knowledge of having provided for future generations.

E. K. Francis: 'The Adjustment of a
Peasant Community to a Capitalist Economy'

---

*Belief in the economic benefits of tourism to poverty-stricken Ireland has a long pedigree. The first issue of the *Irish Tourist* in June 1894 declared on its first page its hope 'to attract multitudinous visitors to annually sojourn at our health and pleasure resorts, and thus leave with us that historic "plethora of wealth", which might act as panacea for Ireland's ills'. James Healy wrote in 1968: 'Tourism is beginning to leave money in the town. It has a nest of very good brown trout rivers ... the drainage may yet give it a summer run of salmon. Fishing is free. The optimist will grasp at these developments as straws in a new significant wind' (*The Death of an Irish Town*, Cork: Mercier, 1968, p. 53).

profits is in opposition to traditional values which give priority to the family home. The Michaels' parlour is turned into a dining room; the old kitchen becomes a sitting room; the new kitchen is built to a scale which sets it far beyond family needs. The bed-and-breakfast sideline is transformed into the hotelier's trade. It is extremely significant that most of the Michaels' visitors stay for a week or two, coming to Inishkillane for their holidays.

In the summer evenings, his house full of tourists, Michael often takes a glass of whisky with his visitors. Although many of them delight in the talk and song of the local bars, Michael greets his visitors on their return from the bar but only drinks with them in the privacy of his own home. In this he makes an identification with the visitor, but shows that he does not need their reassurances. He assumes that he 'speaks their language', and feels he can equally assume that they approve of him and his activities. There can be little doubt that Michael feels superior to the vast majority of local householders, and thinks of himself as someone of another and more advanced mentality. While the local people tend to see visitors as representatives of another and superior culture or consciousness, Michael feels that he shares the consciousness of the tourist. He enjoys a glass of whisky and some conversation with those who come from the cities to pay for room and board in his house.

Michael's enterprises are not restricted to shop and tourist trade. He also operates the only local taxi service. In the isolation of Inishkillane the importance of a taxi service is great: twelve miles from a bus and the closest market town, eighty miles from a railway station: there are always people in need of transport from the parish to 'town'. Few parishioners have cars of their own. The lanes over the hills are so little used that even for a short journey hitch-hiking can take a long time. The need for a taxi service is increased further by the mobility arising from a long history of emigration. Young men and women coming home for visits usually take a taxi for some considerable part of their journey; returning migrants are often met at airport or station by a group of relatives who frequently hire one or two taxis for the expedition. Then there are dances in the local villages; in the summer months a dance takes place every week in one or other of the local village halls. For the young who have a great enthusiasm for these dances, the going and getting home again is always a difficulty. The taxi service does a good business, meeting all these demands for transportation.

Michael owns two cars and a minibus. The journeys he makes vary from the few miles across the parish to over a hundred miles to cities with railway stations and airports. Michael himself has to travel to the city at least once each week, and often has a passenger or two paying to go with him on the journey. As a matter of routine he meets the train from Dublin before setting off for home again, collecting visitors or migrants who want to travel to Inishkillane. The minibus is mainly used for taking the local young people to and from all the dances in the district.

This taxi service is kept busy, and fares are not low. It is a significant part of the Michaels' Inishkillane enterprises. Even when he was obliged to travel twice a week to a city as part of a job on the county council – and received expenses for the journey from the council – Michael charged each passenger £3 to travel with him. There is no competition in the area, and a sizeable demand. Michael Ryan is the only householder in Inishkillane with a service for sale. Though it does not happen in Inishkillane, it is not uncommon for small farmers in the west to rent out a tractor and trailer to the neighbours for occasional jobs.* But in those cases the tractor is basically employed on the home farm; it is not purchased for renting. There is a crucial difference between the hiring of one's own machinery to neighbours in need

* An example of this kind of renting was given in Chapter 4 above.

and investing in machinery *because* of the profit accruing to hire. Only the second is entrepreneurial. Michael Ryan's minibus has no purpose other than the taxi service. It was bought to be a taxi, and its purchase came from a calculation of returns from hire against outlay.

As a local man Michael Ryan inherited the family farm. He has neither sold it nor allowed it to lie fallow. To the relatively small farm which he inherited, Michael has added three other large pieces of land. He has a share in the large areas of the rough mountain country which is in fee as commonage. He owns over two hundred acres and has grazing rights on as much again. The enlargement of land by purchase is encouraged by the Irish Land Commission as part of the continuing endeavour to achieve a fundamental consolidation of holdings in the west, so Michael Ryan is not unique in his attempts to augment the family land. But the scale on which he has done this certainly is unusual. The rent and rate records are dotted in recent years with changes in ownership following his deals with other Inishkillane farmers.

Perhaps his single and most revealing deal was with a local bachelor. This man, well into middle age, had remained on the land and maintained as best he could his family's sixty-acre farm. Eventually the onerous life of an isolated farmer and Michael Ryan's wish to buy the farm resulted in the elimination by sale of the family holding. But the bachelor did more than sell the

---

It is an old story that nearly all the best land in Ireland is in the possession of bullocks.... So human beings withdraw, with some grumblings, but still for the most part courteously, to America, in order that cattle may come in and possess the land with their idle strength and the will of God be accomplished.

Robert Lynd: *Social Life in Ireland*

---

land – he also sold the home he was living in, the outhouses around him, everything. The agreement at the sale included his entitlement to continue living 'at home'. Of course he had money in the bank after the deal, but he had no entitlement, even if he had any willingness, to farm the land which was no longer his. Instead, he was taken on by Michael as an odd-job man around the shop and land. In one sale the man alienated both his land and his labour, while Michael bought farm and worker; traditional tenacious adherence to family land was replaced in one deal by occasional labour for the owner of the farmhouse itself.

Just as the extent of Michael's farm land is unusual, so is the style in which it is farmed. Unlike more traditional farmers in the district, Michael Ryan does not have a mixed farm with a few milk cows, fattening beasts, some hens, a pig, a garden of vegetables, a field or two of winter feed – he has no milk cows, no pigs, and grows no vegetables. The entire farm is for fattening cattle. He buys calves, ranges them on his land, and markets them as bullocks and heifers when the prices seem right. He does not undertake any farming which entails the farming life: there are none of the routines of monthly, seasonal, yearly round in Michael's farming. His is not the agriculture of subsistence; it is remote from the family farms whose commitment to a definite social form is almost as strong as their commitment to a particular farm.

Michael Ryan farms exclusively for the market; his farming is simply a business. The size and shape of his farm are regulated according to business possibilities and requirements. Farming itself is subordinated to profit. This activity and the conceptions behind it, formed by considerations totally at odds with or simply outside the traditional life style, distinguishes the Michaels' farm from virtually all others around. Where his neighbours use the market to buttress the family farm, to ensure the continuity of the essentially traditional styles, in some

---

The threat to the small farmer, the large-scale economic unit, specialized production by means of the internal combustion engine and bags of chemical or simply the theory of agriculture to the financial wolves, cheap food on the debt system, etc., etc.... they can all be boiled down to one thing – the separation of the people from the soil.

H. J. Massingham: *Wessex Letters*

---

harmony with the mentality of subsistence of peasant farming, Michael Ryan finds in the marketplace the one and only compelling rationale for farming at all.

In owning two small boats, Michael Ryan is apparently implicated in another traditional activity. The boats are used for inshore lobster fishing. But Michael's own role is indirect and his relationship to the fishing is once again entrepreneurial. He occasionally takes a boat out into the bay on a calm summer evening, and fishes with a hand line for mackerel. He does not fish commercially, and never does the lobster fishing himself. Instead he gives the use of a boat, outboard motor and tackle to a fisherman farmer living some two miles along the coast. The use is given in return for a share of profit from the catch. Michael is no fisherman and has no interest in baiting pots, hauling lines, storing live lobsters, or risking the hazards which lobster fishing entails. Without any of these activities, with no risk to self or equipment, and independent of his like or dislike for hours spent on the sea, he can still gain from a good fishing year and be sure that a local resource is not entirely excluded from his business life.

As shopkeepers, hoteliers, taxi drivers, with interests in farming and fishing, this wide-ranging entrepreneurial family is kept constantly busy. Behind all this activity there lies a distinctive mentality. Their life style is not tempered by the opposite moods of winter and summer, nor formed by the changing demands of seasonal work, nor underpinned by a commitment to family farm and lands, nor bedevilled by changes which are undermining the traditional styles and conventions, nor pained by the isolation these changes are bringing with them. Equally, the Michaels' consciousness is at variance with the consciousness of the more traditional and confused of Inishkillane. Attention to money is commonplace enough, even in the remotest communities of rural Ireland, but single-minded preoccupation with profit is rare indeed. All farmers must today give some thought to the viability of an undertaking, all are in some degree mastering the ways and wiles of the marketplace, but the large majority assume within their marketing activities a need for community. In the last resort this need is met by a show of goodwill to the man with whom the deal is being effected, a drink in the bar to clinch it, the ancient tradition of giving a penny with every bargain, the very lack of haste – these things are aimed at the obviation of hostility. Behind them lies a concealed assumption that dealing is inimical to friendliness, and therefore to community. The more developed and widespread such practices are, the less ascendant the pure motive of profit; again they are clues to a traditional mentality.

There are clues enough, however, to the lack of entrepreneurial consciousness among the vast majority of Inishkillane householders. Their reluctance in co-operation, the retention of

---

By the way, the husband was a wonderful gentle-mannered man, for we had luncheon in his house of biscuits and porter, and rested there an hour, waiting for a heavy shower to blow away; and when we said good-bye and our feet were actually on the road, Synge said, 'Did we pay for what we had?' So I called back to the innkeeper, 'Did we pay you?' and he said quietly, 'Not yet, sir.'

W. B. Yeats: *Synge and the Ireland of his Time*

---

family farming, their demoralization itself, all testify to a great indifference to the fiats of profit-making. Those who do have a strong inclination towards the entrepreneurial world and have assumed its mentality, for the most part leave. The move is right enough: capitalism and the commitment to any particular place or activity are mutually inimical. Moreover, the distinctiveness of the Michaels' mentality is evidenced in the relation with other people in the parish. The social distance between Michael and his neighbours has already been suggested, but despite it the Michaels are obviously well known, much discussed, and heavily relied upon. In their central position in the community's economy, as suppliers of many goods that have become virtual essentials or keenly desired, they are, at least indirectly, in continual touch with the people of Inishkillane. But the attitudes which parishioners display towards the Michaels vary greatly. By some they are remorselessly criticized, by others esteemed worthy of boundless respect and praise.

Most simply, the two poles of opinion represent a division in the community which follows the division between the two groups concentrated on shop and bar. The young who are decided upon emigration, who do not think of themselves as central members of the local farming life, who are displaced either by role, status or their own free decision from the traditional continuities of life on the land, are most sympathetic to the Michaels. Implicitly their approval is signalled by the time they spend in and around the shop. More directly they enjoy telling strangers about the great successes of the shop family. It is striking how many of the local girls and younger women delight in detailing all the splendour of the Michaels' home, telling the colour of each new coat of paint, estimating the cost of every innovation. And among the 'shop crowd' such conversation is not critical, or jealous, or in any apparent way touched with resentment or hostility. Rather the successes embodied in the Michaels' home and business life are vicariously attained by the approvers. Their identification with the Michaels is a corollary of their sense of participation in a more urbane and 'enterprising' consciousness.* In detailing the achievements of one who exhibits that consciousness *par excellence* they affirm the success and vitality of the consciousness itself. To these people the Michaels constitute a reassurance and affirmation of their social and moral stance. From this flow praise and approval.

By the same processes, those who are centred on bar and farm are less enthusiastic about the Michaels and their activities. Hostile opposition or resentment are not expressed very easily or openly to strangers. It is assumed, of course, that tourists and visitors coming from cities will incline towards respect for the Michaels. The first minutes of any conversation about them between a local farmer and an outsider are laden with circumspection and testing. Typically, the opening remarks involve mention of some success of the Michaels, some symbol of his style. 'It's a fine big house they have,' says the local farmer, waiting for the implications of tone and detail contained in a reply. Behind this cautious beginning lie both hostility towards the Michaels and a strong desire to enlist visitors' support in the criticizing.

But it doesn't do to be always looking for money. There was Whaney the miller, he was always wishing to dream of money like other people. And so he did one night, that it was hid under the millstone. So before it was hardly light he went and began to dig and dig, and he never found the money, but he dug till the mill fell down on himself.

A County Clare woman, quoted by Lady Gregory in:
Visions and Beliefs in the West of Ireland

---

*One very revealing comment on Michael was made to me by one of his local supporters: 'He's very diplomatic. You can say anything to him and no one any the wiser. Oh, he's a very good businessman.' See the discussion of gossip and privacy in Chapter 5 above.

But there are strong feelings of antipathy which must out. A fire in Inishkillane on Easter Sunday of 1967 cast its light on much of the hostility felt towards the Michaels. On a bare acre of land at the edge of the village, Michael planted a small copse of evergreen trees. In a district singularly lacking in trees this tiny planting was conspicuous. On that Easter Sunday night the trees caught fire and half were burnt down. Significantly enough, it was automatically assumed that someone had put a match to the trees. Michael and the Gardai attempted to discover the culprit. The Gardai asked people for information, and eventually heard that a man had been seen walking up the village street on the night of the fire, in the direction of the trees, carrying a can of paraffin oil. The man was duly questioned, and he pointed out that he was on his way home from the shop where he had bought the oil that afternoon. When describing the questioning this man was extremely indignant. He insisted on several things: he did not start the fire; he would have been delighted to have started the fire; he had a 'fair idea' of who did start the fire; but he for sure was not going to tell the Gardai or anyone else anything about it. The men in the bar listening to the declaration showed their full agreement: they would all have enjoyed burning those trees. They had all been pleased by damage to Michael's property. Even if the fire was started by wind or leprechaun, there was no question as to where loyalties lay among the householders in the bar.

To this incident can be added the range of issues on which criticism and complaint are made to turn. There is an issue of allegiance to political parties: Michael is active in Fianna Fáil; many of the men in the bar protest a commitment to Fine Gael. Householders often insist that the tide of opinion in the countryside around Inishkillane is running fast against Michael Ryan's chances should he be thinking of becoming a Fianna Fáil candidate. Then there is the recurrent complaint against the prices charged in the shop. It is asserted that things are much cheaper and of a better quality in some other shops in some other places. And the charges made to guests for bed and board and to everyone for the taxi are cited as further evidence of the Michaels' harsh business practice. These allegations are compounded by complaints about the low wages paid to the girls who help in shop and guesthouse – complaints, it is worth noting, made more vociferously by parents than by the employees themselves. Similarly, the plight of the odd-job man whose farm Michael bought gives cause for anger against the shop family. There are indeed few elements of Michael Ryan's business which are *not* criticized and resented by householders of the parish.

But there is a more general complaint made against the Michaels by the men in the bar. They do not like the way the Michael Ryan family all work in harmony in the interests of the business. Michael in fact has two brothers in business in nearby towns, and the three help each other as much as they are able. It is this co-operation, extended beyond the occupants of one household, upon which resentments often settle. I have argued that refusal to join with others in pursuit of economic improvements is an important element in the overall trends towards isolation of households and reduced interest in farming itself. And the Michaels are the exponents of the new mentalities within which these important trends find their significance and coherence. Isolation is both viable and desirable for the farm householders because of a series of factors: they have discovered in remittances and relief monies a functional alternative to co-operation; they have a sense of the futility of farm life in a milieu where few marriages are taking place and where no new generation is being prepared for the future; they place a high valuation upon the integrity of each household, a value deeply ingrained by tradition. The Michaels, however, have set themselves apart from these considerations. They would certainly not be satisfied by the minimal security the remittance offers, and would see dependence on relief or any other subsidy as failure. But they do have a clear sense of the advantage the situation provides to the effective businessman. Theirs are not the traditionally inscribed values. The new entrepreneurial family finds no difficulty – symbolic, emotional or material – in co-operating with relatives in advancing their economic interests.

Many Inishkillane farmers express opposition to the mentality behind this co-operation. They are attacking the entrepreneurial mind. It is in this context that the issue of relief and its potentially inhibiting effects on enterprise and economic development can perhaps be resolved. The Michaels *do* have enterprise, are industrious, and in a capitalistic sense are 'progressive'. The men who lean heavily on relief and remittances are not. But the difference between Michael and so many of the other house-holders resides more basically in their mentalities than in their economic lives.

Michael's economic life is underpinned by a distinctive consciousness. So are the economic lives of others. In describing a socio-economic system, it is always necessary to examine how economic practice and social consciousness cohere.* Thus there

---

The vivid sense of cash displayed by the grocer was a grievous offence against Bulgat ideas of town talk.... To talk of money is an impropriety. To reveal excessive desire *for money is – Allah defend us – an impiety.*

Daniel Lerner: *The Passing of Traditional Society*

---

* It follows from this theoretical precept that change in a moral framework can only take place in the wake of change in socio-economic circumstances which ultimately created and nourished it. I am aware of the difficulties which culture, contact and information theories cause to that argument (see introductory chapter). But a moral framework *can* outlive its coherence and can thereby become an important part of a complex of ambiguity, ambivalence and confusion. It is possible to subscribe to a form of historical materialism without becoming committed to a trite or patently false sociology of knowledge.

is a coherence between the mentality and the economies of those householders in Inishkillane who depend on remittances and relief. If these were taken from them, they would no more become attuned to a more capitalistic or entrepreneurial economic mode than they would suddenly find within themselves a knowledge of book-keeping. An Inishkillane bachelor farmer, deprived of his cash earnings, would be no more able to become a shopkeeper than Michael Ryan, if deprived of his business interests, would be happy to be a traditional subsistence farmer. In all senses, their minds are on what they do. The propounders of the view that relief and remittance corrode the will and undermine the economy are simply ignorant of the nature of social life, are not willing to grasp the intricate connection between mentality and life-style. Michael Ryan's critics are the men who do not have a mind for business and feel hostile to its ways. And those filled with approval for him have a mind to be like him. It is perhaps the tragedy of the west of Ireland that there can be no reconciliation between the two. His friends leave, and his critics see out the tradition which holds them on its last and fraying strings.

In his somewhat limited interaction with other Inishkillane people, Michael Ryan is inclined to be abrupt and assertive. There is an air of officiousness about his dealings in the shop which evokes even if it does not necessarily presuppose a sense of superiority. Like many busy men, Michael Ryan seems authoritative. As a locally important businessman he has established and justified in the eyes of outsiders, many Inishkillane parishioners, and probably himself, a basis for authority.*

*Patrick Gallagher in the 1930s came to the realization that the shopkeepers were going to dominate the countryside: 'The *gombeen* men will be your politicians and bosses of the future.' Although the struggle he describes in *Paddy the Cope: My Story* (Jonathan Cape, 1939) was largely against outsiders, he astutely quoted A. E.'s remark that *gombeen* men had always done well in the poorest districts.

Predictably enough, this air is resented by bar people and accepted by the shop people. In the more routine dealings with shoppers Mrs Michael has by far the greater contact with local people and is acknowledged to be by far the most personable member of the family. In his more reclusive role, Michael Ryan can perhaps afford to pay scant attention to the niceties of social life, but these 'niceties' have their place in traditional country life, its needs and its communality. Householders are hospitable and kindly, even if the vigorous social life and economic co-operation in which kindliness and hospitality have their most vital place are much atrophied.* Michael Ryan, as a house-holder, establishes his social position and moral orientation through his public behaviour. His abruptness and authoritative-ness, therefore, seem to connote his family's social domi-nance.

Michael's eleven-year-old son Patrick is remarkably aggres-sive towards other children in the parish. He goes to the local school, yet has an extraordinary authority over his schoolmates. Unlike his sisters, who in being unusually shy and subdued are in a different way quite separate from their peers, the son is confident and assertive almost to the point of being something of a bully. Other boys like to go with him to help Michael with the cattle, but when they go they are given orders by the young son. It is as if the son discovers with other boys the attitudes his father adopts towards other householders. Perhaps most poignant of all, the bar family next door have a son called Tommy who is slightly younger than Patrick. Tommy loves to spend time with Patrick, and is constantly finding reasons for running next door

*The stranger's welcome is especially significant in this context, and much can be discovered in the country people's goodwill to out-siders (see Chapter 1 above). Julian J. Greifer has written: 'The attitude to the stranger is one of the barometers which marks the growth in ethical refinement and sensibility of a community' ('Attitudes to a Stranger', *American Sociological Review*, 10, 1945, p. 739).

to play. But this 'play' invariably takes the form of helping: Patrick tells Tommy what to do, and with the mercilessness of childhood never hesitates to pass on to Tommy all his more onerous chores. Tommy is sent to fetch a stray bullock off the hillside, is told to go down to the Post Office to get a 'message', to hurry round after tea to help tidy the yard. Most of all Tommy likes to be with Michael Ryan, and will hear no complaint against him. In his submissiveness before the authoritative demands of Patrick, Tommy's behaviour might be interpreted as a sign of the child's preference for shop over bar, and his acceptance of the Michaels' right to dominate.

The traditions of Irish peasant life evidently do not encourage a hierarchical community. Indeed, a corollary to the value of farm-family independence is the absence of any such inter-family authority structure. The powers of vested authority came either from outside, in the form of landlords and colonists, or from people of specialized education and role, in the form of priests, teachers, and most recently solicitors. More generally, the authorities in rural Ireland constitute a distinctive class, occupationally or nationally far removed from local farm life. The community itself therefore tends to be one group with more or less identical life-styles, backgrounds and economic interests. The consciousness of this group, insofar as it included a sense of

---

I was but a little child with my little book going to school, and by the home there I saw the agent. He took the unfortunate tenant and thrun him in the road, and I saw the man's wife come out crying and the agent's wife thrun her in the channel, and when I saw that, though I was but a child, I swore I'd be a Nationalist. I swore by Heaven, and I swore by hell and all the rivers that run through them.

A local politician quoted by
John B. Yeats in: *With Synge in Connemara*

---

common identity, was formed by difference from, opposition and often resistance to the sources of established social authority.

Class-consciousness among farm families of rural Ireland was discussed in the *Limerick Rural Survey*. There it was concluded that 'status is directly related to the class ladder and indirectly to emotional and moral evaluations of individuals and groups'. But in Limerick, according to the *Survey*, there are numbers of farmers who hire labour. It is noted that many of the farmers assiduously maintain the difference between owner and labourer in the details of daily farm life.* In that situation, where hiring of labour is widespread, the class system will have a more certain place. But in Inishkillane, as in the vast majority of parishes of the west of Ireland, there are status differences – of which the farmers themselves are sole arbiters – but not class differences: all householders are in the same relation to the means of production, even if they benefit in different degrees from that relation. Where all are small farmers, conceptions of social class have no place. In the society I have been describing, the nearest equivalent to class consciousness in regular social life is to be found in status based on family assessments. The

---

In so far as millions of families live under economic conditions of existence that separate their mode of life, their interests and their culture from those of the other classes, and put them in hostile opposition to the latter, they form a class. In so far as there is merely a local interconnection among these smallholding peasants, and the identity of their interest begets no community, no national bond, and political organization among them, they do not form a class.

Karl Marx: *18th Brumaire of Louis Bonaparte*

---

* The *Survey* reports for example that many farmers would not eat dinner at the same table as their workers, often dividing their kitchen with a screen to enforce the separation (pp. 209 ff.).

Inishkillane people would not have any answer to questions like: what social class are you and what class are the Michaels? Such questions presuppose an idea of social relations which is not to be found in these districts and which, despite local people's appreciation of class consciousness among urban people, has made barely any intrusion into the attitudes and organization of their own social structure.

Yet it is true that the Michaels have a distinctive economic ascendancy within the community, do have a form of life and a corresponding set of social relationships which separate them both materially and morally from all other local families. All the information in this chapter points to that simple conclusion. And there is a sense in which this ascendancy can be seen as a matter of socio-economic class: they do occasionally hire labour, and more generally they use their resources in a way quite outside the traditional perimeters of economic life.

But the Michaels' advantage depends upon changes in the economic lives of all householders as much as their own unusual way of exploiting these changes. The two factors turn on the part played by money in the community. The importance of cash received via remittances and social welfare payments has already been pointed out. Obviously, the demoralized community spends a large proportion of all those earnings on the provisions and services on sale at the Michaels'. In many peasant societies, money was allotted by source to certain definite ends. Thomas and Znaniecki, in their account of the Polish peasantry, noted this phenomenon in some detail: there, money from the sale of a cow was saved for large spendings, like dowries and festivities; money from the sale of eggs was pin-money and spent on small daily needs; money from dowries was used for buying land or cattle.* This apportioning of money to definite purposes on account of its source suggests the immensely

* W. I. Thomas and F. Znaniecki, *The Polish Peasant in Europe and America*, New York, 1927, pp. 1138 ff.

developed sense of position or function in peasant society. It also suggests the strength of control exercised over every part of the economic life.

Today these mechanisms have faded away almost entirely. The decline of family, the end of rigid conventions organizing both persons and things into well-defined functions and according to accepted ends, the erosion of faith in the older ways, the overall demoralization of the people, have all changed the way money is used. Families have not incorporated money into their old social system. Instead, a substantially new system has been formed on the *basis* of money. At the economic centre and social apex of the new system are the Michaels. And in some degree, both critics and supporters of the entrepreneurial family are implicated in this system. It is everyone's money that the Michaels' business depends on, because everyone has come to depend on money.

The Michaels are virtual monopolists. In very many small parishes of Ireland there is an entrepreneurial family with striking economic and social ascendancy. In some ways the entire fabric of social life in these remote rural communities indicates the passage to a more capitalistic social form. The entrepreneurial family represents the culmination of this trend. The spending habits of Inishkillane people are an important element in their uneasy and often transitional social and moral predicament. Yet the position of the entrepreneur depends upon this spending and the social situation underlying it. His business success relies upon the endemic disposition towards consumer spending and service dependence. The bar people buy most of what they need to maintain their farm lives and their insulation; the shop people buy all they need including many symbols of participation in the larger and perhaps more open centres to which they will be moving. This spending is a corollary of the people's demoralization: they do not consider competing with Michael, do not hope to fulfil their more obviously urban expectations in the countryside, rarely associate rural life with a full life. Resignation of the householder and emigration of the young further guarantee the entrepreneur's position. It must remain a mystery how it comes about that one family, locally born and with the same broad social experience and of the same religion as other parishioners, can so completely adopt this distinctive mentality and develop an independent economic life. Moreover, among their neighbours this mentality and economic life cause ambivalence and confusion rather than any desire to emulate. I am not able to point to any sociological or economic factors which urged this distinctive role on the Michaels. Yet from a sociological point of view the entrepreneurial family appears a natural and crucial element in the plight of rural Ireland. Its success is a reflection and consequence of the changes which have been occurring in the countryside, changes deriving from other and earlier changes which gave rise to the traditional peasant society itself.

The place of the entrepreneurial family may seem remote from traditional life, but it is part of a country's final acquiescence in urban capitalist culture. The peasant community of farm families and the new entrepreneur are now socially, economically, and ideologically intertwined. They comprise between them the essence and the index of demoralized rural Ireland.

Bibliography

This bibliography concentrates on the literary, sociological and historical books about Ireland. Also included are a number of community studies and technical essays which provided useful comparative material and some valuable theoretical perspectives.

Aalen, F. H. A., 'A Review of Recent Irish Population Trends', *Population Studies*, 17, 1963–4, pp. 73–99

Aalen, F. H. A. and Brody, Hugh, *Gola: The Life and Last Days of an Island Community*, Cork: Mercier, 1969

Alspach, Russell K., *Irish Poetry from the English Invasion to 1798*, Philadelphia, 1943

Anderson, R. and T., *Vanishing Village: A Dutch Maritime Community*, Seattle, 1964

Anon., *Tales of Irish Life*, London: Robbins & Co., 1824

Anon. ('A Guardian of the Poor'), *The Irish Peasant, A Social Survey*, London, 1892

Anon., *Real Life in Ireland by a Real Paddy*, Methuen, 1904

Arensberg, Conrad M., *The Irish Countryman*, Macmillan, 1937

Arensberg, Conrad M. and Kimball, Solon T., *Family and Community in Ireland*, Harvard University Press, 1968

Banfield, Edward C., *The Moral Basis of Backward Society*, Chicago: Free Press of Glencoe, 1958

Barrow, John, *A Tour Round Ireland*, London: John Murray, 1836

Becker, B., *Disturbed Ireland*, London, 1881

Beckett, J. C., *A Short History of Ireland*, London, 1952

Beckett, Samuel, *Murphy*, London, 1938

Behan, Brendan, *Hold Your Tongue and Have Another*, Hutchinson, 1963

Behan, Dominic, *Ireland Sings*, London, 1965

Beinem, H. Van, *The Morale of the Dublin Busmen*, Tavistock Press, 1964

Bell, N. W. and Vogel, E. F. (eds.), *The Family*, London, 1961

Birmingham, George A., *The Lighter Side of Irish Life*, New York: Fred Stokes, 1912

Birmingham, George A., *Irishmen All*, New York: Fred Stokes, 1913

Butt, Isaac, *Irish People and Irish Land*, Dublin, 1867

Callwell, J. M., *Old Irish Life*, Blackwood, 1912

Campbell, J. K., *Honour, Family and Patronage*, Oxford University Press, 1964

Carleton, Will, *Traits and Stories of the Irish Peasantry*, Dublin, 1830

Cobbett, William, *A History of the Protestant Reformation*, Sydney, 1956

Commission on Emigration and Other Population Problems, Dublin, 1956

Connell, K. H., *The Population of Ireland, 1750–1845*, Oxford University Press, 1950

Connell, K. H., 'Peasant Marriage in Ireland After the Great Famine', *Past and Present*, 12, 1957, pp. 76–92

Connell, K. H., 'The Land Legislation and Irish Social Life', *Economic History Review*, 2nd series, XI, 1, 1958, pp. 1–7

Connell, K. H., 'Peasant Marriage in Ireland – Its Structure and Development since the Famine', *Economic History Review*, XIV, 3, 1962, pp. 502–23

Connell, K. H., 'The Potato in Ireland', *Past and Present*, 23, 1962, pp. 57–72

Connell, K. H., *Irish Peasant Society*, Oxford University Press, 1968

Coyne, William P. (ed.), *Ireland Industrial and Agricultural*, Dublin: Dept of Agriculture, 1909

Dalton, G. (ed.), *Tribal and Peasant Economies*, New York, 1967

Davies, E. and Reese, A. D., *Introduction to Welsh Rural Communities*, Cardiff, 1960

Descamps, Paul, *Le Portugal: La Vie Sociale Actuelle*, Paris, 1935

Drake, M., 'Marriage and Population Growth in Ireland 1750–1845', *Economic History Review*, 2nd series, XVI, 2, 1963, pp. 307–13

Lord Dufferin, *Irish Emigration and the Tenure of Land in Ireland*, London, 1867

Edwards, R. Dudley, and Williams, T. Desmond (eds.), *The Great Famine*, Dublin, 1956

Ellman, Robert, *James Joyce*, Oxford University Press, 1959

Emmett, Isabel, *A North Wales Village*, Routledge & Kegan Paul, 1964

Evans, E. Estyn, *Irish Heritage*, Dundalk, 1949

Evans, E. Estyn, *Irish Folk Ways*, London, 1961

Farrell, Michael, *Thy Tears Might Cease*, London: Arrow Books, 1963

Flower, Robin, *The Irish Tradition*, Oxford University Press, 1947

Flower, Robin, *The Western Island*, Oxford University Press, 1947

Fox, J. R., 'Structure of Personal Names on Tory Island', *Man*, 192, 1963, pp. 153–5

Fox, J. R., 'Kinship and Land Tenure on Tory Island', *Ulster Folklife*, 12, 1966, pp. 1–17

Fox, J. R., 'Tory Island' in B. Benedict (ed.), *Problems of Small Territories*, London, 1967, pp. 121–6

Francis, E. K., 'The Adjustment of a Peasant Community to a Capitalist Economy', *Rural Sociology*, 17, 1952, pp. 215–26

Frankenberg, R., *Village on the Border*, London: Cohen & West, 1957

Freeman, T. W., 'The Changing Distribution of Population in Donegal', *Journal of Statistical and Social Inquiry Society of Ireland*, 16, 1940–41, pp. 31–46

Freeman, T. W., *Pre-Famine Ireland*, Manchester University Press, 1957.

Gaeltacht Report, Dublin, 1926

Gallagher, Patrick, *Paddy the Cope: My Story*, Jonathan Cape, 1939

Gladstone, W. E., *Speeches on the Irish Question*, London, 1886

Lady Gregory, *Visions and Beliefs in the West of Ireland*, 2 vols., Putnams, 1920

Greifer, Julian J., 'Attitudes to a Stranger', *American Sociological Review*, 10, 1945, pp. 739–45

Habakkuk, H. J., 'Family Structure and Economic Change in Nineteenth-Century Europe', in Bell and Vogel, q.v., pp. 374–86

Healy, James N., *The Death of an Irish Town*, Cork: Mercier, 1968

Henry, R. J., *The History of Sinn Fein*, Dublin, 1920

Humphries, Alexander, *New Dubliners*, Routledge & Kegan Paul, 1966

Jackson, John A., *The Irish in Britain*, London, 1963

Jackson, John A., *Report on the Skibbereen Social Survey*, Dublin, 1967

Jackson, Kenneth, *Studies in Early Celtic Nature Poetry*, Cambridge University Press, 1935

Johnston, J. J., *Irish Agriculture in Transition*, Oxford University Press, 1951

Kavanagh, Patrick, *The Green Fool*, Michael Joseph, 1938

Kavanagh, Patrick, *The Great Hunger*, Dublin, 1942

Kavanagh, Peter (ed.), *Dictionary of Irish Mythology*, New York, 1959

Kimball, Solon T., *Tradesman and his Family*, Harvard, 1935

Klein, Josephine, *Samples of English Culture*, 2 vols., Routledge & Kegan Paul, 1964

Kropotkin, Prince Peter, *Mutual Aid*, Penguin Books, 1939

Larkin, Emmet, 'Economic Growth, Capital Investment and the Roman Catholic Church in Nineteenth-Century Ireland', *American History Review*, LXXII, 3, 1967, pp. 852–84

Le Fanu, W. R., *Seventy Years of Irish Life*, Macmillan, 1893

Lenin, V. I., *The British Liberals and Ireland* (1914), Dublin, 1970

Lerner, Daniel, *The Passing of Traditional Society*, Illinois, 1958

Limerick Rural Survey, Tipperary, 1962

Littlejohn, James, *Westrigg: The Sociology of a Cheviot Parish*, London, 1963

Love, S. (ed.), *Popular Tales and Legends of the Irish Peasantry*, Dublin, 1834

Lynd, Robert, *Social Life in Ireland*, London, 1909

Lysaght, D. R. O'Conner, *The Republic of Ireland*, Cork: Mercier, 1970

MacAmhlaigh, Donal, *An Irish Navvy*, Routledge & Kegan Paul, 1964

MacDonagh, Donagh and Robinson, Lennox (eds.), *The Oxford Book of Irish Verse*, Oxford University Press, 1958

MacDonagh, Oliver, *Ireland*, Prentice Hall, 1968

MacGowan, Michael, *The Hard Road to Klondike*, London, 1962

MacIntyre, A. C., *Social and Moral Change*, Oxford, 1967

Mansergh, N., *Ireland and the Age of Reform*, London, 1940

Marcondes, J. V. Freitas, 'Mutirao or Mutual Aid', *Rural Sociology*, 13, 1948, pp. 374–89

Martin, E. W. (ed.), *Country Life in England*, London, 1949

Martin, E. W., *The Shearer and the Shorn: A Study of Life in a Devon Community*, London, 1965

Marx, K., '18th Brumaire of Louis Bonaparte', K. Marx and F. Engels, *Selected Works*, vol. I, pp. 247–345

Mason, T., *The Islands of Ireland*, Cork: Mercier, 1967

McDowell, R. B. (ed.), *Social Life in Ireland, 1805–1845*, Dublin, 1957

Micks, W. M., *The History of the Congested Districts Board*, Dublin, 1925

Mill, J. S., *England and Ireland*, Dublin, 1868

Mill, J. S., *Chapters and Speeches on the Irish Land Question*, Dublin, 1869

Mogey, J. M., *Rural Life in Northern Ireland*, London, 1950

Mogey, J. M., 'Agricultural Techniques and Progress', *Rural Sociology*, 4, 1955, pp. 240–51

Mullen, Pat, *Man of Aran*, Faber, 1934

Mullen, Pat, *Hero Breed*, Faber, 1936

Mullen, Pat, *Irish Tales*, Faber, 1938

Mullen, Pat, *Come Another Day*, Faber, 1940

Nojan, I. Edward, *The Irish People (Their Height, Form and Strength)*, Dublin, 1899

O'Briain, F., *Rural Depopulation in Ireland*, Tipperary, 1949

O'Brien, George A. T., *The Economic History of Ireland in the Eighteenth Century*, Dublin, 1918

O'Brien, George A. T., *The Economic History of Ireland in the Seventeenth Century*, Dublin, 1919

O'Brien, George A. T., *The Four Green Fields*, Dublin, 1936

O'Brien, John A. (ed.), *The Vanishing Irish*, London: Allen, 1954

O'Casaide, Seamus, *Irish Poems: A Book of Irish and Scottish Gaelic Verse*, Dublin, 1928

O'Casey, Sean, *Collected Plays*, 4 vols., Macmillan, 1949–51

O'Casey, Sean, *Autobiographies*, Macmillan, 1963

O'Crohan, Thomas, *The Islandman*, Oxford, 1951

O'Donnell, Peader, *Islanders*, London, 1928

O'Faolain, Eileen, *Irish Sagas and Tales*, Oxford University Press, 1954

O'Faolain, Sean, *The Irish*, Penguin Books, 1947

O'Faolain, Sean, *Vive Moi*, Rupert Hart-Davis, 1965

O'Grady, Desmond, *The Dying Gaul*, MacGibbon & Kee, 1968

O'Mahoney, David, *The Irish Economy, An Introductory Description*, Cork, 1967

O'Suilleabhain, Sean, *A Handbook of Irish Folklore*, Dublin, 1942

O'Suilleabhain, Sean, *Irish Wake Amusements*, Cork: Mercier, 1967

Paul-Dubois, L., *Contemporary Ireland*, Dublin, 1908

Peterson, William, 'A General Typology of Migration', *American Sociological Review*, XXIII, 3, 1958, pp. 256–62

Pomfret, J. E., *The Struggle for Land in Ireland*, Princeton, 1930

Porcupine, Peter, *A Bone to Gnaw for the Democrats*, Philadelphia: Bradford, 1795

Rees, A. D., *Life in a Welsh Countryside*, University of Wales Press, 1950

Ryan, W. J. L., 'Some Irish Population Problems', *Population Studies*, 9, 1955–6, pp. 185–95

Sauvy, A., 'Social and Economic Consequences of Ageing of Western European Populations', *Population Studies*, 2 (1), 1945, pp. 115–25

Saville, John, *Rural Depopulation in England and Wales*, London, 1957

Sayers, Peig, *An Old Woman's Reflections*, Oxford, 1962

Sheehy, Michael, *Is Ireland Dying?*, London, 1968

Smith, Cecil Woodham, *The Great Hunger*, London, 1962

Stacey, M., *Tradition and Change*, Oxford University Press, 1960

Stephens, James, *The Crock of Gold*, London, 1912

Swann, A. P., *The Book of Inishowen*, Donegal, 1938

Swann, A. P., *Romantic Inishowen*, Dublin, 1947

Swift, Jonathan, *Irish Tracts, 1720–1723*, and *1728–1733*, in H. Davis (ed.), *Collected Works*, vols. 9 and 12, Oxford, 1948 and 1955

Synge, J. M., *In Wicklow and West Kerry*, Dublin, 1912

Synge, J. M., *The Aran Islands*, London, 1921

Synge, J. M., *Collected Works*, Allen & Unwin, 1932

Thomas, W. I. and Znaniecki, F., *The Polish Peasant in Europe and America*, 2 vols., New York, 1927

Tuke, James H., *Irish Distress and Its Remedies*, London, 1880

Vayda, Andrew, 'Pomo Trade Feasts' in G. Dalton (ed.), q.v., pp. 494–501

Vidich, A. J., Bensman, J. and Stein, M. R. (eds.), *Reflections on Community Studies*, New York: Wiley, 1964

West Cork Resource Survey, Dublin, 1963

Williams, W. M., *The Sociology of an English Village*, London, 1956

Williams, W. M., *A West Country Village*, London, 1963

Yeats, John B., *Essays Irish and American*, Dublin, 1918

Yeats, W. B. (ed.), *Fairy and Folk Tales*, London, 1888

Yeats, W. B., *Irish Fairy Tales*, Macmillan, 1892

Yeats, W. B., *Synge and the Ireland of his Time*, Dundrum, 1911

Yeats, W. B., *The Irish Literary Revival*, Heinemann, 1915

Yeats, W. B., *Mythologies*, Macmillan, 1959

Index